Disclaimer: The author and publisher have made every effort to place citations with the figures and tables. Anyone who believes that a source reference is missing or incorrect can contact the publisher.

D/2022/45/265 – ISBN 978 94 014 8625 5 – NUR 800

Cover design: Steve Reynders
Interior design: Crius Group
Translation: Alanah Reynor

LannooCampus Publishers is a subsidiary of Lannoo Publishers, the book and multimedia division of Lannoo Publishers nv.

LannooCampus Publishers
Vaartkom 41 box 01.02   P.O. box 23202
3000 Leuven   1100 DS Amsterdam
Belgium   Netherlands
www.lannoocampus.com

WIM VERMEULEN

SPEAK UP *NOW!*

MARKETING IN TIMES OF CLIMATE CRISES

Lannoo Campus

Table of Contents.

PREFACE   9

THE GREAT HESITATION   15
The gods no longer cross lake Suwa   15
When scientists sound the alarm, politicians get to work   16
The Great Hesitation   20
Keep 1.5 alive   23
And yet we have everything we need   26
Mounting protests   29
Growing climate anxiety   35
What are the risks for the business sector?   37
An opportunity for marketers   43
Time to get cracking   49

UNITE BEHIND THE SCIENCE   61
The climate and biodiversity are top priorities   61
The Holocene   64
The planetary boundaries   68
Does climate friendliness sell?   80
Who makes climate-friendly purchases?   84
What about the crisis? What does the future hold?   86
The messaging from scientists is clear   87

BREAKING DOWN BARRIERS   **93**
Affordability   93
Knowledge   95
Ease   118
Not all climate-friendly brands are created equal   126
The climate barrier no-one is talking about   147

SPEAK UP NOW   **155**
Words matter   155
How governments are asking us to adapt our language   157
How consumers are asking us to adapt our language   164
Speak up now   184

ACKNOWLEDGEMENTS   **191**

NOTES   **193**

WHAT OTHERS SAY ABOUT *SPEAK UP NOW!*   **206**

We are already at +1.1°C global warming

The damage is no longer reversible

The Amazon lost 17% from its forest

5 mass extinctions in Earth's history

First chance to stabilise climate again is around 2050

We have 8 years to halve global emissions

Oceans at least 1.5°C warmer

Humanity has wiped out 60% of animal populations

The climate crisis is a race we can still win

Exceeding 1.5°C triggers climate tipping points

A drought warning is in place for 47% of the EU

+12.000 species are threatened

Preface.

" The scientific consensus is clear: we are sleepwalking off the edge of a cliff.[1]

These are not the words of a climate scientist, but those of James Watt, cofounder of BrewDog, the hip and well-known brewery causing a stir in the United Kingdom. His words create a stark mental image that perfectly summarises his conversation with Sir David Attenborough and instantly sets the tone for BrewDog's climate plan.

Watt understands that the focus of BrewDog's business operations must be the climate. He also understands that consumers need to hear this loud and clear, because today they expect companies to take climate leadership. This is confirmed by our own research: 83% of the consumers surveyed are calling on the business sector to take the lead in the climate transition. This is momentous. Never before have so many consumers appealed to companies to solve a social issue. They expect answers, they expect brands and companies to make their voices heard, they expect them to explain how they are tackling the climate crisis. They want businesses to speak up and they want them to do it now. Some companies would rather not do this, they would rather continue with business as normal on the side-lines. That's understandable; most companies would rather not put themselves in the spotlight and certainly not when it comes to the climate. But it's becoming ever more difficult to stay silent, because silence is construed as doing nothing. According to consumers, companies that do nothing to solve the climate crisis are part of the problem. They are the ones that will bear the brunt of the impact in the years to come.

In chapter 1, we'll see why consumers are making this appeal and why it is so important for companies to take this issue seriously. We'll dive into the history of the climate crisis to understand the origins of the Great Hesitation and why we're in the situation we're in today. Seven years after the Paris Agreement was adopted, scientists have to admit that it's highly unlikely we will meet the target of 1.5 degrees Celsius. This means that we will miss our first chance to stabilise the climate by around 2050 and that we'll have to wait until around 2070 for our second chance. This is a massive risk for the business sector because it means that, until 2070, we will have to endure more frequent and more intense extreme weather events. In the meantime, climate fear and protests are multiplying. It's not just young people taking back to the streets following the pandemic. In April 2022, over 1,000 climate scientists took to the streets as part of Scientist Rebellion, chaining themselves to the doors of banks and gas-and-oil companies. Even ex-diplomats, involved in years of climate negotiations, are joining Extinction Rebellion and calling for civil disobedience. If you don't follow the situation closely, you wouldn't believe everything that is happening. And it's all having an impact on consumers. They no longer see the future through rose-coloured glasses. They're losing their confidence in political leaders to guide us safely through the climate transition and are instead looking to the business sector to take the reins. That carries expectations that companies had better take seriously.

Chapter 2 lays out the risks for the business sector and there are quite a few of those. We'll dive into climate science in order to clearly explain what those risks mean. However, the climate crisis also brings with it opportunities. We'll look at how companies can lead the climate charge in different ways and explore with what language and with which voice they can share this with the consumer. Not all companies will have a talent for it. We'll discuss the importance of the uptick in climate-friendly consumption and the decline in consumption of regular products. This switch could cut global emissions by 40 to 70% which, according to some sources, is necessary to achieve the 1.5 degrees Celsius target set out in the Paris Agreement. This is one very important insight from the latest IPCC report that deserves much more atten-tion from marketers and advertising professionals than it is currently getting. Making climate-friendly consumption the social norm is one of the essential conditions to achieve the much-needed emissions cuts. This offers not only an opportunity for growth in the short-term, but can also limit the risks for businesses in the long-term. Making a certain consumption pattern the social norm is right up every marketer's street. We'll look at how climate-friendly companies are already doing this and how they're trying to dismantle the barriers standing in the way of climate-friendly consumption in chapter 3.

Nevertheless, it's not going to be easy, which brings us to chapter 4. Here we will get to the heart of the most pivotal climate barrier for businesses: the climate-friendly claims that companies are making lack credibility. Few consumers believe companies when they talk about their climate-friendly initiatives. This is an important finding of the research we conducted under the leadership of professor Gino Verleye in late 2021. We mapped the cynicism and disbelief shown toward the business sector on topics such as climate friendliness and climate leadership. We presented almost a hundred 'sustainable' advertising campaigns to consumers to sound out how credible they were. The results were staggering. The credibility of companies' climate communications is exceptionally low. We truly are looking at a 'language problem'. The language that marketers speak is that of the old normal, not of the climate normal.

Credibility, in the language of the old normal, is not a problem. If a toothpaste brand promises that our teeth will be sparkling white in no time using their product, nobody would take that tube back to the supermarket after two uses to complain that the company lied. We don't believe that our teeth will ever appear as white as those of the man or woman in the ad. Our expectations are much lower. At most, we just want our teeth to look a little less yellow and we know for a fact that that won't happen overnight. However, when it comes to sustainability, credibility is a key factor in consumers' evaluation criteria. Most importantly, it's the key to making sustainability communication effective. In other words, sustainability communication does not work if it's not believable. We researched what makes climate-friendly communication credible and have been able to identify several key factors. It's clear what type of language consumers expect from us and what criteria it must fulfil. We also know which story lines are better suited to the new climate normal and which aren't.

It's not just consumers who are setting new and higher bars for the language that companies speak in the climate normal; policymakers are also scrutinising how companies communicate their climate commitments. They do not approve of the work they see today. In several European countries, new rules are being implemented for all climate-friendly communications. Those rules leave no room for interpretation: climate commitments must be clear, unambiguous and substantiated. If they're not, firm action will be taken: campaigns are being banned on a regular basis nowadays.

Marketers and advertising professionals have been called 'the architects of desire'.[2] We create demand among consumers for certain products or services. At times, there comes a point when we need to question whether it is socially responsible to keep boosting demand for a particular product. We questioned our practices in the same way when the scientific consensus clearly established the damaging effects of smoking. Is it still socially responsible today to promote products that aren't climate-friendly? Shouldn't we be doing exactly the opposite and putting all our creative strength into speeding up the transition to climate-friendly consumption?

"It was the best of times, it was the worst of times, it was the age of wisdom, it was the age of foolishness, it was the epoch of belief, it was the epoch of incredulity, it was the season of light, it was the season of darkness, it was the spring of hope, it was the winter of despair." That's what Charles Dickens wrote in *A Tale of Two Cities* during the French Revolution. In some ways, it's reminiscent of the world today. For marketers and advertising professionals, it is 'the season of light'. Companies are being asked to take the lead in the sustainable transition that the world needs to embark on. To do that, they need to step out of the shadows and explain what we can do. They have to speak up now. Most companies don't yet speak the language of the new climate normal and that is where marketers and advertising professionals come in. Now, more than ever, they can make a difference but first, they must learn the language.

CLIMATE CRISIS TODAY

We are already at +1.1°C global warming

! Current levels of atmospheric CO_2 have not been experienced for at least two million years.

! 32 years ago, IPCC scientists urged us to take immediate action to reduce greenhouse gas emissions.

! The rate at which CO_2 has increased in the atmosphere since 1900 is at least 10 times faster than at any other time during the last 800,000 years.

! That current 1.1°C temperature rise is already causing disruption to weather patterns.

! The momentum of industrial activity and the delayed response of the atmosphere and oceans mean a further increase to at least 1.5°C warming is inevitable — and many scientists expect 2°C to be breached even if the world takes the strongest action that we can realistically expect.

! Pollution from fossil fuels is killing 8.7 million people every year. That means 1 person dies every 4 seconds because the air we breathe is poisonous.

! According to the IMF, we directly and indirectly subsidise the fossil-fuel industry to the tune of $5.3 trillion annually. That's $10 million every minute.

Oceans at least 1.5°C warmer

Sources

Bottollier-Depois, A. (2022, 18 March). *Three decades ago world told to "act now" on climate*. Phys.Org. Last accessed on 24 June 2022, at https://phys.org/news/2022-03-decades-world-told-climate.html

Cookson, C. (2022, 19 March). *The race to curb global warming*. Financial Times. Last accessed on 24 June 2022, at https://www.ft.com/content/7fb14f50-3308-47dd-8448-28499143d55e?desktop=true&segmentId=7c8f09b9-9b61-4fbb-9430-9208a9e233c8#myft:notification:daily-email:content

Vohra, K., Vodonos, A., Schwartz, J., Marais, E. A., Sulprizio, M. P., & Mickley, L. J. (2021). Global mortality from outdoor fine particle pollution generated by fossil-fuel combustion: Results from GEOS-Chem. *Environmental Research*, *195*, 110754. https://doi.org/10.1016/j.envres.2021.110754

The air we breath is poisonous

The Great Hesitation.

THE GODS NO LONGER CROSS LAKE SUWA

At the foot of the Japanese Alps lies the vast body of water, Lake Suwa. For more than 500 years, Shinto priests have measured the temperature of the water. According to Shinto legend, if they have three measurements of minus 10 degrees during a season, there is a chance that *omiwatari* – 'the God's Crossing' – will occur. At night, you can hear the ice cracking under the footsteps of the god Takeminakata, crossing the lake to meet his beloved, the goddess Yasakatome. In reality, the thundering sound comes from the thick ice cracking due to prolonged freezing temperatures. In the middle of February 2020, Shinto priest Kiyoshi Miyasaki measured the temperature of the water. He was concerned; that winter, he hadn't yet measured any freezing temperatures at all. The *omiwatari* was already becoming a less frequent occurrence. That year, it wasn't going to happen either. The thermometer showed that the water was 5.7 degrees Celsius.

According to Shinto priests' archives, Takeminakata used to cross the lake almost every winter. Since the second half of the 20th century, this has changed considerably. Between 1950 and 2000, there were 22 winters without *omiwatari*; since 2000 there have already been 13. Shinto priests' writings about the *omiwatari* are some of the oldest climate archives in the world, inevitably showing us how quickly the Earth has warmed in the last few decades.[3] The time when the ice cracked under the feet of the gods seems to be gone for good.

Never has a natural phenomenon managed to throw the climate system as off-balance as humankind itself. Even the meteorite that crashed into our planet 65 million years ago didn't have the same impact, even though it cast darkness over the planet for two years and wiped half of all living beings, including the dinosaurs, off the globe.[4] Today we know perfectly well what we're doing and what the consequences of our actions will be. Scientists have spelled it out clearly. Their work speaks volumes. The consequences of the climate and biodiversity crisis will make it ever more difficult to maintain our social structures and wellbeing. That, in turn, has an impact on the business sector. We're making an effort, but we've not (yet) succeeded in obtaining the systemic change that is needed to limit the duration and impact of the consequences of both crises. We're dragging our feet at a time when we should be kicking things up a gear.

WHEN SCIENTISTS SOUND THE ALARM, POLITICIANS GET TO WORK

Scientists have been sounding the alarm for four decades.

A climate scientist first managed to make world news back in 1988 when two leading figures found each other: American senator, Tim Wirth, and NASA climate scientist, James Hansen. Tim Wirth, from Colorado, was elected senator in 1986. In that role, he started to receive more and more concerning reports about climate change; he was looking for a way to bring political attention to the issue. At the same time, NASA climate scientist James Hansen had spent several years studying climate change. In 1981, in an article in the renowned journal *Science*, he predicted that the burning of fossil fuels would lead to a global temperature increase of 2.5 degrees Celsius by the end of the 21st century. That prediction didn't receive much response. This was in the 80s, when America was under the spell of capitalism and the *money-is-everything* mentality, glamorised in films like *Wall Street*. Nobody was interested in a scientist coming to break that happy bubble.

SCIENTISTS HAVE BEEN SOUNDING THE ALARM FOR FOUR DECADES.

———

Seven years later, in 1988, America sweated through a heatwave. The water level in the Mississippi was so low, inland navigation was impossible. Crops were drying up and forest fires took hold throughout the country. Almost half of America was declared a disaster zone. The cover of Time magazine on 4th July 1988 summed it up in three words: 'The Big Dry'.[5] Just at that moment, James Hansen had finished a study with conclusive evidence that the climate was heading in the wrong direction. He was looking for a way to share his research with the wider public. Meanwhile, Senator Tim Wirth wanted to highlight the fact that the heatwave was no coincidence and was the work of humankind. When they came across each other's work, Wirth promised to organise a hearing so that Hansen could share his findings with the people who could do something about it. On 28th June 1988, on the day of the hearing, it was 38 degrees Celsius, the warmest day of the heatwave. It's as if the heat had wanted to give Hansen a helping hand. Waiting to speak before the 'Senate Committee on Energy and Natural Resources' and 15 television cameras about his scientific conclusions, he wiped the sweat from his brow with a handkerchief.

Hansen started his speech by showing that the climate in 1988 was warmer than it ever had been and that the likelihood that these high temperatures were merely a coincidence was no more than 1%. He then showed what many people, with the fossil-fuel industry at the fore, decried: the climate crisis was being caused by humankind and more specifically by the burning of coal, oil and gas. Hansen also gave the senators and the public a glimpse of the future: "In 2029, in 41 years, it will be abnormally warm everywhere in the world and that could have disastrous consequences for our society because there will be more and worse droughts, heatwaves, floods and water shortages. We can prevent this," he said, "but to do that the emission of greenhouse gases must drop drastically." The next day, the New York Times printed on the front page: 'Global Warming Has Begun'.[6] Hansen's message had been delivered. Together with Tim Wirth, they had succeeded in putting global warming firmly on the international community's agenda. Once the alarm has been sounded by scientists, the international community jumps into action. At least, that's the rule. Hansen and Wirth expected their work to be picked up and for a reaction to follow.

The climate issue is not the first life-threatening problem that the global community has had to deal with; the first was the hole in the ozone layer.

That problem was tackled with the clout and speed needed. On that issue, there was no question of hesitation. In 1974, a group of scientists published a study which suggested that the hydrochlorofluorocarbons or HCFCs used in consumer products such as aerosols, packaging and fridges damage the ozone layer. The ozone layer sits 14 to 45 km above the Earth and absorbs most (97%) of the ultraviolet rays emitted by the sun. Ultraviolet rays are dangerous for people, plants and animals. They're dangerous to such an extent that if there were no ozone layer, life on Earth would be impossible.

In 1985, 11 years later, scientific evidence showed that there was a hole in the ozone layer above Antarctica. The international community shot into action. In 1987 in Vienna, just two years later, it was agreed to halve the use of HCFCs. Three years later, in Montreal in 1990, it was decided to completely ban the use of HCFCs in industrialised countries by 2000 and in developing countries by 2010. Today, the use of HCFCs is banned in 197 countries and the ozone layer is recovering, slowly but surely. Any talk of HCFCs threatening all life on Earth is long gone.

The combination of the scientific warning cry and the international community's preparedness to act shows how quickly a global issue can be tackled. Add to that the willingness of several countries to accept rules being imposed on them from above and a business community that actively seeks to offer solutions, and many thought they had found the formula for success to solve all global problems swiftly and effectively. James Hansen's warning to the American senate in 1988 also didn't fall on deaf ears, at least initially. Four years later, in June 1992, 179 countries came together in Rio de Janeiro for the 'United Nations Conference on Environment and Development', better known as the 'Earth Summit'. Everyone was there: 108 Heads of State and Government, 2,400 NGO representatives and 10,000 journalists. The result is well-known: the UN Framework Convention on Climate Change (UNFCCC), better known as the Climate Convention. The world set itself the goal "to combat global climate change by reducing greenhouse gas emissions."[7] The countries present committed to developing national policy plans to reduce greenhouse gas emissions (mitigation) while working together to seek ways in which we could adapt to a warmer world (adaptation). It was also agreed that they would meet yearly at a COP, or Conference of the Parties, to ensure that sustained progress was being made. You'd think they were ready to get cracking.

THE GREAT HESITATION

But then began the Great Hesitation. In 1997, nine years after Hansen raised the alarm, the yearly COP meetings led to the climate conference in Kyoto. There, the EU and 164 other countries signed the Kyoto Protocol, pledging to reduce greenhouse gas emissions by 8% between 2008 and 2012. In 2001, the first flaws in the agreement started to show. The American senate didn't want to ratify it, even though Al Gore had played an important role in the development of the agreement and President Clinton had signed it. Then US President George Bush thus withdrew from the agreement, to which he also had strong objections. His main concern was that the Protocol only imposed commitments on industrialised countries and not on developing or newly industrialised countries such as China, India and Brazil. They were already generating considerable amounts of emissions while the emissions cuts imposed on the US would have a severe impact on the coal industry. At that time, the US was dependent on coal for half of their electricity supply. Reducing emissions would cause not only a hike in electricity prices that would affect millions of Americans, but could also lead to millions of lost jobs. Those risks were too great for a president to take. The Kyoto Protocol thus entered into force without the US. Seeing as the US was responsible for a third of global CO_2 emissions at that time, everyone knew the agreement was dead in the water.

In 2005, COP11 was held in Montreal. It was the largest international gathering since the implementation of the Kyoto Protocol. By then, everyone knew that the Kyoto Protocol wouldn't bring us any closer to achieving our goal. Global greenhouse gas emissions were still climbing unchecked. There was no willpower for a new agreement or for stricter reduction targets. The only decision that was taken was to buy some time and extend the Kyoto Protocol until 2012.

The next large conference was in December 2009 in Copenhagen. All the international community could do was come to the same conclusion as in 2005: greenhouse gas emissions were still rising in various countries. Meanwhile, scientific reports showing the negative impact of emissions on the climate were piling up. You would think that, at this point, the international community would start putting serious pressure on countries to convince them to mitigate that negative impact. Instead, the conference entered the history books as 'Flopenhagen'. No consensus was reached for further reduction targets. It was a severe blow to the hope that one day a plan would be adopted to tackle the climate crisis together and end the Great Hesitation. Images of a world marked by extreme weather events, political conflicts over water and food, and social conflicts over the ever-worsening economic situation suddenly became very real. Someone had to get matters back on track.

Christiana Figueres is the daughter of Jose Figueres, leader of the Costa Rican revolution who came to power in 1948. Christiana was 12 when her father became president for the third time. She spent part of her childhood growing up in the presidential palace and the rest on a coffee plantation her father owned. Her father taught her her life motto – "Impossible is not a fact, it is an attitude." She is proud to be the daughter of a revolutionary. "I'm very comfortable with the word revolution," she said. "In my experience, revolutions have been very positive."[8] In 2009, six months after the disastrous summit in Copenhagen, she was asked to be the architect of a new climate agreement as the executive secretary of the UNFCC. Everyone, herself included, knew that this climate agreement would be our last chance. If she didn't succeed in getting 195 countries to agree in 2015, we had no chance of curbing the climate crisis. That was the consensus. It thus became her responsibility to save the planet, but she didn't have any authority: every country is sovereign. She was enthusiastic, but not really optimistic. When asked at her first press conference if she thought a new climate agreement was feasible, she answered: "Not in my lifetime."[9]

In the meantime, climate scientists kept sounding the alarm bell, including in the fifth IPCC report published in 2014. The IPCC, the Intergovernmental Panel on Climate Change, is a UN organisation that was created to give the international community and its policy makers regular updates on the scientific state of climate change. They publish a report every six years, the result of the work of hundreds of scientists who base their work on tens of thousands of other scientific reports. The conclusions of the report thus force the international community to face the facts. All their agreements and attempts to convince various countries to do something about greenhouse gas emissions have served no purpose. The concentration of greenhouse gases – especially CO_2, methane and nitrogen oxide – in our atmosphere is now higher than it has been for the last 800,000 years. According to scientists' calculations, we're on track for warming of 3.7 to 4.8°C compared to pre-industrial levels (the level before the industrial revolution began). The world will become a very difficult place for humans to survive. Everyone agrees on that.

Finally, 40,000 people, including 147 Heads of State and Government, were expected to attend the summit on 30th November 2015 in Paris. Security measures at COP21 were high. Just two weeks earlier, Paris had been the target of several terrorist attacks. Three terrorists blew themselves up at the Stade de France, while another group shot at people seated on restaurant and café terraces and another set forced entry into the Bataclan concert venue and shot at the crowd. It was the most deadly attack France had seen since WWII and the deadliest in the EU since the attack in Madrid in 2004. Several people called for COP21 to be called off but Figueres and Laurent Fabius, the French minister of Foreign Affairs, stood their ground.

Two weeks later, on 12th December, 200 negotiators hugged and congratulated each other in the hall of the conference centre at Le Bourget airport. Fabius ended the COP21 just before 7.30pm with good news. The Paris Agreement had been concluded. Figueres had succeeded in getting the world to take action. The Great Hesitation was over. The aim of the Paris Agreement was to limit the global temperature increase due to the climate crisis to no more than 2 degrees Celsius compared to pre-industrial levels. Furthermore, they wanted to do everything they could to limit warming to 1.5 degrees. The strategy was to halve emissions by 2030 and to reduce emissions to net-zero by 2050. No specific climate goals were imposed. Every country was to define their own targets in what was named 'Nationally Determined Contributions' or NDCs. The culmination of all NDCs would determine whether we could truly tackle the climate crisis. At the time of signing, ambitions were admittedly not high enough to limit global warming to the agreed 2 degrees or less; rather, they would lead to warming of 3 degrees by the end of the century. However, the negotiators counted on countries setting ever more ambitious targets. In order to provide the world with some assurances, it was agreed that countries would revise their NDCs every five years and, if needed, step them up a notch. The next meeting would have been in 2020, but we all know that the COVID-19 pandemic interfered with that. As a result, the first overview didn't take place until 2021 at the climate summit in Glasgow.

KEEP 1.5 ALIVE

COP26, held in November 2021, was the most important climate summit of the decade because it was our last chance to limit global warming to 1.5 degrees. That's how the United Kingdom, the organiser of the event, put it thus raising the stakes considerably. They weren't wrong, it was indeed our last-chance summit. The UN didn't call this decade 'The Decade of Action' for nothing. But many negotiators would have preferred it to sound less ambitious. Imagine if the negotiations had only achieved half of what they had set out to achieve, like in Copenhagen which was a painful flop. How negative would public reaction have been? Enough time had passed for the euphoria of the Paris Agreement to subside, instead leaving room for overwhelming disappointment and growing protests.

Countries had to submit their climate ambitions or NDCs by 30th July 2021. It soon became clear that not everyone had done their homework. Only 113 countries sent in new or adapted NDCs. Together, those commitments represented a reduction of 12% in global greenhouse gas emissions by 2030 (compared with 2010). It seemed that we were starting to get somewhere. But if all NDCs were added up, including those of countries that had not submitted an update, the result was an increase of no less than 16% by 2030. An increase that meant that limiting climate change to one and a half degrees was no longer possible. Warning bells sounded once again.

One month later, on 8th August, a new IPCC report was published. It was the first of three in the 2021-2022 cycle. UN Secretary General, Antonio Guterres, named it the "code red for humanity". Its contents were clear: we need to shift up not one, but two gears if we want to have a hope of achieving the 1.5 degree scenario. It wasn't just the content that was the cornerstone of this report; the language used left no room for misunderstanding. "This is the world's scientists screaming at the top of their lungs," said Michael E. Mann, one of the world's greatest climate scientists. It was clear that the scientific community was no longer restricting itself to simply giving figures and recommendations. They hadn't yet joined the protests taking place in the streets, but the message to policy makers was the same: you must finally start taking responsibility – it's urgent. The international negotiators knew what they needed to do.

The start of the climate summit brimmed with hope. World leaders were flown in to give speeches accepting full responsibility for themselves and the negotiators, peppering their talks with imperative language. Some of them made the news, including Barak Obama's speech, but that had less to do with the content of his speech than his status as a political rock star. Mia Mottley, the prime minister of Barbados, also made the headlines with her speech that chilled the audience to the bone. "1.5 is what we need to survive. Two degrees, yes Secretary General..." she said looking at Guterres, "is a death sentence for the people of Antigua and Barbuda, for the people of the Maldives, for the people of Dominica and Fiji, for the people of Kenya and Mozambique, and yes, for the people of Samoa and Barbados. We do not want that dreaded death sentence, and we have come here today to say: Try harder!" She talked about the countries on the frontline of climate change, countries that have a negligible impact on the causes of climate change but are particularly vulnerable to the consequences, countries that would be uninhabitable if warming were to reach 2 degrees. The importance of limiting the planet's temperature rise to 1.5 degrees couldn't have been any clearer.

During the first few days, it seemed that the political world had understood the message and was going for gold. Even representatives from the business sector were present. There had never been so many of them present. The largest delegation was from the gas-and-oil industry, which was a cause of concern for many who feared that they weren't there to roll up their sleeves. Mark Carney, banker and former governor of the Bank of England, immediately gave an unmistakable signal that the business community had understood the urgency. As the UN Special Envoy for Climate Action and Finance, he had negotiated with the financial sector and ensured that they were also committed to the 1.5 degree target. When he took to the floor, he said: "Today the money is there, the money is there for the transition, and it's not blah blah blah." He was speaking on behalf of 500 financial institutions that would align 130 billion dollars – roughly 40% of the world's financial assets – with the 1.5 degree target. In other words, all those financial institutions were committed to ensuring that the environmental impact of all their investments, loans and financial transactions would not have an impact larger than that allowed for under the 1.5 degree target.

By saying "and it's not blah blah blah", Carney was referring to Greta Thunberg's speech at a protest gathering of Youth4Climate in Milan a few weeks earlier. In her speech, she called out political leaders and the business community: "Build back better. Blah, blah, blah. Green economy. Blah blah blah. Net-zero by 2050. Blah, blah, blah. This is all we hear from our so-called leaders." On the big screen behind her, you could see the president of COP26 listening. In contrast with Carney, he remained completely expressionless during Thunberg's speech. Nevertheless, other than striking out at an eighteen-year-old, Carney's message was clear: only drastic efforts matter now and the financial sector is ready to act. But the first cracks soon appeared. By the end of the first week, Greta Thunberg already felt disappointed. At a Friday For Future protest, she dubbed the summit "a global greenwashing festival". As for the negotiators, we started receiving the first messages saying that the negotiations were more complex than expected. Moreover, the promises made by the business sector, as well as those made by Carney, were analysed in detail by various NGOs which found a number of serious gaps. The initial hope of the beginning of the conference started to fade.

After that, if any progress was being made we didn't know about it. There was just silence. That didn't necessarily mean bad news; there's lots of hard work going on behind the scenes at a climate summit. However, just before the end, when normally we would be dotting the i's and crossing the t's, China and India drew a line in the sand on the phasing-out of coal production. They didn't agree with the target of halting all coal production. It was a highly unusual move that didn't attract much sympathy from other countries. Given that time was running out to get negotiations back on track, both countries got their way. The other negotiators felt extremely frustrated. Alok Sharma, the president of the climate summit, apologised for what happened in his closing speech. "I understand the deep disappointment, but I think as you have noted, it's also vital that we protect this package." Next came an image that has travelled around the world: he paused, but not to catch his breath. He held a finger in front of his mouth for an instant, enough for us to understand that he was fighting back tears. It's an image of such sincere disappointment that speaks volumes: the climate summit didn't achieve its purpose. They didn't manage "to keep 1.5 alive".

Subsequent analyses showed that 1.5 degrees could still be in reach but that another year was needed to get everybody on the same page. This will be at the climate summit in November 2022, COP27 in Egypt. Nevertheless, those estimates don't take the speed at which the climate crisis is evolving into account. On 4th April 2022, during the press conference on the last IPCC report in the 21-22 cycle, the scientists burst that bubble: "Unless there are immediate and deep emissions reductions across all sectors, 1.5°C is beyond reach."[10] Unless we pull the plug on the use of fossil fuels straightaway, the 1.5 degree target is no longer attainable. The problem is that 80% of our global energy use comes from fossil fuels.[11] We can't pull the plug right now. In other words, seven years after the Paris Agreement was signed, we know that the most important objective, limiting warming to 1.5 degrees, is no longer realistic. We are going to surpass that target. That means that we need to focus on dropping back below that level as quickly as possible instead, which makes everything much more difficult and complex. The fact that we can't keep up with the speed at which the climate crisis is unfurling became even clearer on 10th May 2022 in an article in the Financial Times. The news hit us like a bomb: "The world is increasingly likely to experience global warming of 1.5C within the next five years." Between now and 2027, the likelihood is high that we will experience a year when we reach that 1.5 degree mark. Nobody had predicted that. The prospect that we would reach 1.5 degrees of warming within the next five years was zero just seven years ago. That gives you an idea of the breakneck speed at which the climate crisis is unfolding. What the British head researcher declared is perhaps the most concerning of all: "If we're going to keep to 1.5C, that may be difficult now."[12] The damaging effects of our hesitation are now far too close for comfort.

AND YET WE HAVE EVERYTHING WE NEED

Today, we are living in a world that is 1.1°C warmer than it was before the start of the industrial revolution. We can clearly feel the impact that it's having. India recorded its warmest month of March since the country's meteorological service started records 122 years ago. In March 2022, the average temperature across the whole country reached 33.1°C, surpassing the 32.7°C of March 2021, the second-warmest March ever. Sunil Das, a rickshaw driver in Noida on the outskirts of Delhi, is no longer able to work after 10 in the morning. "I head back home after 10 and resume in the evening when the heat has subsided a bit," he said in an interview with a local magazine.[13] "It has reduced my earnings but what alternative do I have?" Sunil is not the only one suffering as a result of the climate crisis. Sapna Verma, HR supervisor at an IT company, said that she didn't expect the consequences of extreme heat to be so tangible. One afternoon, after she dropped her son off at a friend's house two kilometres away on foot, she had to go and lie down on her bed.

"For about an hour I had no energy. I was sweating profusely and extremely irritable, in no mood to talk to anyone."[14] Nikhil Dey, who works with Indian villagers in Rajasthan, explains that women there are striking because they want to start their day at 5am rather than 7am, so that they can complete their hours before it gets too hot.[15] "The states of Punjab, Haryana and Uttar Pradesh − the breadbasket states of the country − all reported a 10-35% drop in yield due to the early onset of summer and the excess rainfall seen in December and January.[16]" Dry winds on the North-Indian plains, that led to uncharacteristic farm fires, affected production even further. India had a chance to make up for the drop in global wheat supply, after Russia invaded Ukraine on 24th February 2022, but couldn't because of the damage caused by the climate crisis.

The impact is also being felt on the other side of the world. Los Angeles is experiencing what scientists call a megadrought: a period of drought that lasts longer than normal. Due to water shortages, the city's authorities are on the point of imposing a total watering ban. "This is a crisis unlike anything we have ever seen before," Deven Upadhyay, chief operating officer of the Metropolitan Water District of South California, told anyone who was listening in April 2022. "Normal will not work."[17] California is dependent on snow and rain at the beginning of the year in order to store enough water. This year, the first three months were the driest they've ever had. Consequently, California only has a little more than half of the water it needs to get through the rest of the year. In mid-April 2022, district officials in the Los Angeles region issued an emergency water shortage order for the first time in its history. "What we didn't know was that it was going to come this fast," said Rebecca Kimitch, a spokesperson for the water company. "We are having to adapt in real time."

Temperatures are also rising closer to home. In June 2022, the temperature in Madrid hovered around the 40 degree mark for more than a week. Schools closed in the afternoon, outdoor sports events were cancelled, life in the city fell quiet because it was too hot to even do your errands. Record temperatures are also being reached elsewhere in Europe. The summer of 2022 was one of the driest ever in Europe, a continent that scientists say is warming faster than the global average. Forest fires spread rapidly across the continent, burning more than 4.6 times the average area of forest fire seasons over the last 19 years, while Alpine glaciers melted at a record pace. A drought warning is in place for 47% of the EU and a drought alert for 17% of the EU, a historic first.[18] Throughout the world, the climate crisis is raging at full strength. And clearly there are victims: every year, roughly 5 million people die from the impact of the climate crisis.[19] For comparison, just over 6 million people died from COVID-19 worldwide between March 2020 and April 2022.

The latest IPCC report – the one that concluded that limiting warming to 1.5 degrees would only be possible if we pull the plug on fossil-fuel use immediately – also calculated what our current efforts, plans, commitments and regulations by both governments and the business sector would achieve. If we fulfil our current promises, our planet would still warm by 3 degrees, an increase we may already reach by the last quarter of this century. Most of humankind would struggle to survive in a world that's three degrees warmer. We asked Johan Rockström, director of the Potsdam Institute for Climate Impact Research, what a world at 3 degrees would look like while we were making the documentary *The Decade of Action*. His answer was as clear as it is terrifying: "If we come to 3 degrees or even beyond 3 degrees, I call that very simply the catastrophe point. You would have at least 10 but more than 20 metres sea level rise. You would have probably 3 billion people who would be living in areas that are physically no longer possible to host human beings, you would simply not be able to cope because of the levels of temperature. You would have populations concentrating in the Arctic and Antarctic and you would get huge population movements. It's very questionable how we could feed humanity because we would lose so much land that we would end up in a situation where we simply have a planet no longer in a state to support humanity."[20]

Rockström is not the only one who is aware of this reality. The whole political world knows it too. Every single IPCC report comes with a summary specifically designed for politicians and policy makers; it's called 'The Summary for Policy Makers'. Admittedly, just because a summary is published doesn't mean that it is read, but this summary can only be published if all 195 countries approve it. It is thus negotiated at the highest level. The latest 'Summary for Policy Makers' was actually published a few days later than planned because there was some political debate among countries about the wording. In the end, politicians signed a document stating that their prolonged hesitation is the reason why the world will no longer be able to support human life by the end of the century. Yes, you're reading that right. But that's not all. The same report also clearly stated that we have everything we need to tackle the climate crisis and meet the 1.5 degree target. And you guessed it, politicians signed that too. Michael Mann, one of the most respected voices in the climate debate, spoke plainly when he said: "The solution is already here. We just need to deploy it rapidly and at a massive scale. It all comes down to political will and economic incentives."[21]

MOUNTING PROTESTS

How many times do scientists need to sound the alarm for the Great Hesitation to be knocked on the head? Nobody knows. For the time being, we don't see any end in sight so protests are mounting. More than 1.4 million people took to the street in more than 2000 cities for the first Global Climate Strike on 15th March 2019.[22] 7.6 million people participated in the climate protests in 4500 locations across 150 countries during the Global Week for Future in September 2019.[23] One million people joined Earth Day protests on 22nd April 2021 despite the coronavirus pandemic. The same happened a year later on Earth Day 2022. Growing climate protests are not a one-off situation and they're a signal not just to politicians but also to the business sector. Research has shown that the protest in March 2019 negatively affected the stock market value of various European carbon-intensive companies.[24]

This fits into a broader trend of protests. Recent research has shown that the number of protest movements around the world has more than tripled in less than 15 years.[25] According to the authors of the report, we are at a crossroads similar to those in 1830-1848, 1917-1924 and the 60s. The cause is a growing democratic deficit; people no longer feel like politicians are listening to what they are asking and the problem is not what they are asking. "The vast majority of protests around the world advance reasonable demands already agreed upon by most governments. People protest for good jobs, a clean planet for future generations, and a meaningful say in the decisions that affect their quality of life," says Sara Burke, one of the authors of the report[26]. The problem is thus clearly the (lack of) political will to listen.

The climate genie has been let out of the bottle and no-one can get it back in. This is also demonstrated by stories shared in response to protest tweets. On 9th April 2022, when XR (Extinction Rebellion) organised a massive protest in London, Laurence Hill tweeted: "Well, I'm on my first ever protest, at 50. Not sure what to expect, wish me luck". He's no climate activist. He's a man who is concerned about the living conditions of future generations and who has

CIVIL DISOBEDIENCE IS A MORAL RIGHT

decided to do something he's never done before: protest. Among the more than 200 messages of support, Claire B writes: "Go Laurence, I might take after you. Am same vintage, it's time." It's time. That's exactly why climate protests are growing, throughout society and across the whole world.[27]

Even though the wider public is already taking to the streets, the fact that climate negotiators are also calling on people to protest speaks volumes. In the hope that they can have a greater impact for humankind, negotiators are standing side by side with 'rebels'. Christiana Figueres, the woman who led the Paris Agreement negotiations, predicted the rise of civil disobedience in her book *The Future We Choose* and her podcast *Outrage and Optimism*: "Civil disobedience is not only a moral choice, it is also the most powerful way of shaping world politics." For a diplomat who succeeded in getting world leaders to agree to almost halving global CO_2 emissions by 2030 and reaching net-zero by 2050, this is a surprising step. It says a lot about her lack of trust in the correct implementation of the Paris Agreement.

Farhana Yamin is another influential diplomat who has dared to take that leap. Yamin is an internationally-renowned environmental advocate and adviser to developing countries and small island states in the climate negotiations. She is also one of the main authors of the IPCC report and an architect of the climate agreement in Paris. The idea or concept of net-zero by 2050 exists thanks to her. She began to lose her trust in international diplomacy when Donald Trump announced his plans to withdraw from the Paris climate agreement. In 2018, she joined Extinction Rebellion to lead the political team. A year later, she was arrested during an XR protest at the Shell offices in London. "Everyone should have 'activist' on their C.V.," she said about the incident.[28] Both diplomats no longer believe that international diplomats and politicians are capable of tackling the climate crisis in the necessary fashion, namely as the utmost priority for humankind. In order to do this, the climate movement must have as great an impact as that of the civil rights movement in the 60s or that of the suffragettes at the beginning of the last century. It looks like it will because another prominent group recently joined the protests: scientists.

"1.5C is dead. Climate revolution now!" This slogan was visible all around the world on 6th April 2022, the day on which scientists definitively opted for civil disobedience. A thousand scientists from 25 countries united as part of Scientist Rebellion, protesting in capital cities across the world. In Los Angeles, they handcuffed themselves to the entrance of a bank. In Germany, they pro-tested in front of the Ministry for Economic Affairs and Climate Protection. In the UK, they united in front of the Shell PLC headquarters. They pasted documents on government buildings in Mexico, occupied the headquarters of an oil-and-gas company in Italy and threw fake blood at the façade of the National Congress in Spain. Their evaluation of the political actions that are currently being taken is scathing: they're completely insufficient and, worst of all, those who concluded the climate agreements aren't even following through on them. "Unless those best placed to understand behave as if this is an emergency, we cannot expect the public to do so," they wrote in the open letter that they published on protest day.[29] One scientist who succeeded in spreading the message around the world was Peter Kalmus. Kalmus is a climate scientist working for NASA, where he studies the effects of climate change. He knows all too well what awaits us and cannot understand why politicians aren't making it a top priority. According to him, it is completely realistic to expect wars to be waged over remaining water supplies and mil-lions of people to die by the second half of this century as a consequence of extreme heatwaves in cities across the world.[30] "It is my job to say that it is not too late to act, but also to reveal that society is on a terrifying course. I do this out of compassion, especially for young people, in an attempt to change course," he said.[31]

On 6th April, he chained himself to the doors of the JPMorgan Chase building in Los Angeles. He knew that it was only a question of time before he was arrested and that he was therefore putting his career at NASA at risk. Nev-ertheless, he wanted to speak out. His words were so chilling that the video travelled across the world on TikTok and Twitter in no time. In his improvised speech, he said: "I'm willing to take a risk for this gorgeous planet and…," he paused, covered his eyes with his hand and sniffed, "…my sons." With tears in his eyes and his voice breaking, he continued: "We've been trying to warn you guys for so many decades that we are heading towards a catastrophe. And we are being ignored, the scientists are being ignored. And it's got to stop. We are going to lose everything. And we are not joking, we are not lying, we are not exaggerating."[32] The helplessness that shows through his words is terrifying. This man knows what is coming, he knows what needs to happen but he feels as if he is screaming into the abyss. The fact that scientists have joined the climate protests is a watershed moment. After all, there's a code isn't there? Scientists report their findings, politicians interpret them and businesses implement them. But there comes a point when enough is enough. Scientists have now reached that point. Jan Rotmans, a Dutch climate transition expert, explained: "Given that politicians have failed, for decades now, to properly tackle climate change, as a climate scientist you have the right, the moral duty even, to become an activist."[33]

Nobody is holding back anymore, especially since the latest climate report and the message that the 1.5 degree target is no longer achievable,. Christiana Figueres told Bloomberg: "I'm lacking words for this. It's beyond immoral. It's suicidal."[34] The Secretary General of the United Nations, Antonio Guterres, spoke categorically: "Some government and business leaders are saying one thing – but doing another. Simply put, they are lying. And the results will be catastrophic."[35] Alongside Peter Kalmus, a number of scientists are holding policy makers to account in the press. Emma Smart, a British ecologist, was arrested at a protest where she and some other scientists pasted scientific reports about the climate crisis on a government building and glued herself to the glass frontage. She was charged with criminal damage, although what criminal damage she actually caused with her actions is unclear. When she was released, she asked who the criminal really is: "A scientist calling out a government's inaction that will be responsible for a +3°C world, a world in which humankind cannot survive, or a government that prefers to silence those scientists by putting them in jail rather than listening and ensuring that their people do not have to endure a 3°C world."[36]

Judges in the UK have heard the same reasoning before. Katie Dowds, 28, a member of Christian Climate Action and a local church community, took part in a 'Just Stop Oil' protest on Friday 15th April 2022 to demand that the British government put an end to new grants for gas-and-oil projects in the United Kingdom. She was arrested and spent Easter Sunday in a jail cell, waiting for her appearance in court on Easter Monday. When the judge allowed her to speak, she gave a very moving statement: "It is usually a criminal offence to break the window of a house without cause. However, if the house is on fire and there are people trapped inside, such actions are not only proportionate but necessary. Your Honour, our house is on fire and we're doing everything we can to non-violently sound the alarm to save as many lives as possible. According to the UN Secretary General, Antonio Guterres, climate activists are sometimes portrayed as dangerous radicals. But the truly dangerous radicals are the countries that are increasing production of fossil fuels. Investing in new fossil-fuel infrastructure is moral and economic madness. I repeat, Your Honour, that these are the words of the UN Secretary General. Nonetheless, I do plead guilty to the offence with which I am charged. However, I also humbly suggest that it is not concerned, ordinary citizens like myself who should be appearing in court today, but those who continue to profit from, protect and prop up the fossil-fuel industry. Thank you for your time."[37] More and more people are feeling the same way.

Luckily, climate activists aren't the only ones being taken to court. Sofia Oliveira was 16 when she, along with her brother and five other young people from Portugal, filed a case against 33 countries with the European Court of Human Rights. She demanded that governments do more to cut their emissions and safeguard their future physical and mental wellbeing. When asked why she was doing this, she answered: "I've been worried about climate change for a long time. When I was 11 years old, my younger brother André had a terrible asthma crisis. The weather was hot and dry, and he was suffocating. One of the most important reasons I'm involved in this case is to help my little brother have a good future, along with my parents, myself and the next generation."[38] The 33 countries tried to have the case dismissed, but they didn't succeed. On the contrary, the Court decided to handle the case, which was brought to them in 2020, quickly. The ruling, to be made in 2022, will be legally binding and oblige European governments to step up their emission reductions and address their overseas contributions to the climate crisis, including the global emissions of multinational corporations. These seven young people aren't the only ones going through the courts to hold governments to account. Norwegian climate activists filed a lawsuit against their government with the European Court of Human Rights to put a stop to the planned extension of oil-and-gas exploration in the Arctic region. The British government has a number of ongoing cases, including one under the Human Rights Act: the right for young people to life and family life. The Polish government was taken to court five times in 2021 by citizens due to their "regressive" climate stance. In Belgium, on 17th June 2021, the government was found guilty of negligence in its management of the climate crisis. The court ruled that "by refraining from taking all necessary measures to prevent the effects of climate change detrimental to the lives" of the plaintiffs, the government was in breach of its obligations under the European Convention on Human Rights.[39]

The powder keg's fuse has been lit and it's getting shorter and shorter. For a while, it was feared that the global pandemic, with its lockdowns and restrictions, would water down the climate protests. That's obviously not been the case. As the protests keep growing, so does climate anxiety.

GROWING CLIMATE ANXIETY

In the 60s, psychologists Martin Seligman and Steven Maier did an experiment on the helplessness of dogs. For the first test, dogs were administered an electric shock after hearing a certain sound. The dogs were unable to flee so had to experience the shock. In a second series of tests, the dogs were given a means of escape. The psychologists expected the dogs to flee when they heard the sound but to their amazement, they didn't. The dogs looked helpless as they waited for the shock. Seligmann and Maier reasoned that the animals had learned that their fate was no longer under their control, to such an extent that they didn't even take the opportunity to escape. Seligman and Maier called this phenomenon 'learned helplessness'.

The same behaviour was observed in humans. People who have experienced numerous events beyond their control believe that nothing they can do would make any difference. As a result, they display symptoms of stress, apathy and fatalism. Although concepts such as 'learned helplessness' and 'personal control' naturally have an effect on individuals, they are also applicable to groups of people and even to whole communities. A community can collectively believe that they are not in a position to bring about change and, as a result, they stop trying. The results of the Munich Security Index 2022 show us that we have reached that point in the climate crisis today and that is very worrying. Nearly six in ten (57%) people who live in a democratic country feel helpless when it comes to global problems such as the climate crisis. In Italy, 60% of the population feel this way while in Germany and France, it's a little over half (54%). The research for our book, *De Duurzame Belg,* revealed that 67% of Belgians believe that we can no longer control the climate crisis. 72% of the general public in developed countries admit to worrying that they will experience personal damage due to climate change during their lifetimes.

In 2021, the University of Bath conducted a global study of teenagers and people in their 20s which showed that three-quarters of them are worried about the future because of the climate crisis. Just under half (45%) say that their daily lives have already been affected. The most shocking figure is that half (56%) think that "humanity is doomed" and 40% say they don't want to have children for this reason.[40] They're also not impressed with politics: nearly six in ten young people feel that the government is betraying them and future generations by taking too few measures.[41] Meanwhile, scientists are finding it difficult to put their emotions aside. For the "Is this how you feel?"

project, climate scientists were asked to write a letter about how they feel about the climate crisis. The analysis showed that negative feelings prevail and are expressed with words such as 'angry', 'annoyed', 'anxious', 'worried', 'upset' and 'furious'.[42]

The need for information is growing with the rise of protests and anxiety. Google searches for 'climate anxiety' soared by 565% last year (table 1). People also started looking for more answers following the publication of the last IPCC report. They want to know what rising sea levels mean for them (+1000%) and better understand what they can do to tackle climate change (+2600%). According to Google, sharp hikes like this are extremely uncommon.[43]

TABLE 1

Global search trends for many climate-related phrases rose sharply in 2021	
"climate anxiety"	+565%*
"map sea level rise"	+1,000% in the week following the IPCC Report**
"what can I do about climate change"	+2,600% in the week following the IPCC Report**

*Search data compares interest from Aug 2020 – Aug 2021 with Jan 2004 – Aug 2020
**Search data compares interest from week of 8/9/2021 with Jan 2004 - 8/8/2021

Whether we receive emotional support is another question. In a study of news presenters who wrote or talked about the 2021 IPPC report on 25 of the most-linked news sites, 79% reported feeling concerned, anxious, helpless or overwhelmed. Of these, 10% spoke with a neutral undertone, 6% noted some hope and only 5% alluded to a solution. This was also confirmed by an Ipsos study done in November 2021, in which the majority of the more than 20,000 respondents (62%) agreed that they hear a lot more about the negative consequences of climate change than about the progress being made to limit its effects.

Research by the Grantham Institute shows that for every person physically affected by a disaster, 40 are psychologically affected.[44] Let's put this into perspective by looking at what the IPCC report said about the number of people who are currently affected by climate change and how many will be in the future. Currently, one in three people is exposed to deadly heat stress and this is expected to rise to 50%, possibly 75%, by the end of the century. Half of the world's population is already contending with severe water shortages. In total, 3.5 billion people are already very vulnerable to the effects of climate change. Those are just a few figures from the report, but they say enough. If for every person who has to endure the physical effects of extreme weather, 40 more feel the psychological impact thereof, we are headed for global climate depression and an unprecedented extent of learned helplessness. That's not just a guess, it's a certainty. We already know for sure that we are going to experience more frequent and more intense extreme weather events. The same can be said for the consequences.

WHAT ARE THE RISKS FOR THE BUSINESS SECTOR?

In May 2022, Stuart Kirk, the global head of responsible investing at HSBC's asset management division, gave a presentation at a FT Moral Money event. The title of his keynote was: "Why investors need not worry about climate risk". During his speech, he attacked speakers on the podium who had warned the business leaders in attendance about the dangers of the climate crisis. He compared them to the doomsayers who had alerted people about the millennium bug (the one it was feared would cause our computer systems to fail as we entered the new millennium). "That never happened." He also didn't think it would be a shame if Miami were underwater by the end of the century. "Amsterdam has been six metres underwater for years and it's a beautiful place." He defends the idea that the climate crisis won't turn out to be as bad as some make it out to be and that humankind would easily be able to regain control if there were any problems. The bank suspended him two days later. The man had kicked up a bit too much dust with his strong words. HSBC is often blamed and accused of greenwashing. The last thing they want is to be seen as climate sceptics.

FIGURE 1

Most severe global risks over the next ten years (%)

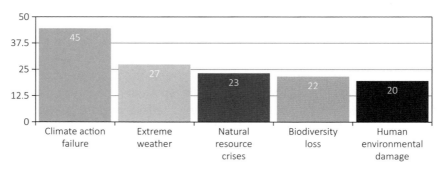

Source: World Economic Forum Global Risks Perception Survey 2021-2022

Luckily, not everyone thinks like Stuart Kirk. In a recent WEF survey, pub-lished in January 2022, there seemed to be a consensus in the business sector about the most pressing risks of the next ten years.[45] The top five risks were all to do with the climate and biodiversity crisis (figure 1). Failure to act on the climate came first, followed by the negative consequences of more and more extreme weather. In third and fourth place were different aspects of the biodiversity crisis. The fact that the biodiversity crisis is so high on the agenda is good news. It's a less well-known crisis, but just as important. These two crises – climate change and threats to biodiversity – could throw our Earth system out of balance and pose a threat to the survival of humanity. More about that later.

The risks of the climate transition for businesses have already been researched in depth. They can be divided into two categories: physical and transition risks.

The **physical risks** include the adverse impact of more frequent extreme weather events: flooding, hurricanes, drought, heatwaves, cold spells, forest fires and so on. The impact can range from damage to or destruction of private or public infrastructure, disruptions to the supply of raw materials or to the distribution to points of sale, disrupted travel for employees and so on. These risks are different for every company, but if you take the time to think about it, anyone can come up with a copious list of potential physical risks, in particular for international companies whose supply chain spans several countries.

FIGURE 2

European versus global temperatures 1850-2019
(degrees Celsius difference compared with pre-industrial levels)

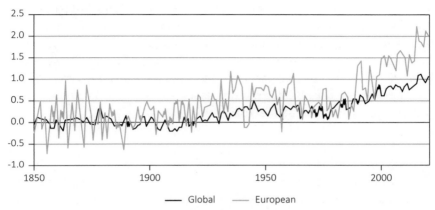

Sources: Annual Global (Land and Ocean) temperature anomalies – HadCRUT (degrees Celcius) provided by
Met Office Hadley Centre observations datasets.
Notes: Temperature anomalies are shown compared with the pre-industrial period between 1850 and 1899.
The observation is for 2019.

In order to be able to foresee these physical risks, it is important to understand that we will experience extreme weather events until the middle of
this century. Any measures we implement today will only affect the climate
after the middle of the century. If we succeed in reducing our emissions to
net-zero by 2050, the temperature will only stabilise to 1.5 degrees after that
date. There is nothing we can do to bring the climate crisis under control
before then. Bearing this in mind, companies must think about everything
that could go wrong between now and 2050 and make sure that they are
ready to handle it. The IPCC released an interactive online atlas last year to
help with this task (https://interactive-atlas.ipcc.ch). Companies can use this
tool to see which types of extreme weather event will occur most frequently
and in which locations, so that they can understand what might happen in
various climate scenarios.

European companies have to take an additional factor into consideration:
the average temperature in Europe is higher than the global average temperature. This has become abundantly clear in the last decade. As we can
see in figure 2, the average temperature in Europe has risen by 1.9 degrees
compared to pre-industrial levels while the rest of the world has warmed by

1.1 degrees Celsius. When we talk about a global temperature increase of 1.5 degrees, the temperature in Europe will soar above 2 degrees. If we head toward a global temperature increase of 3 degrees, that would make it more than 5 degrees warmer in some parts of Europe. The fact that we're currently on the path to a global increase of more than 3 degrees is not just particularly bad news for companies in Europe, it's also something that few companies are taking into account when creating their investment plans. Exactly how warm it will be in Europe and when can be checked on the IPCC's interactive atlas. In addition to the physical risks, there are the **transition risks**. We can categorise these risks in four groups: policy and legal, technological, market-disrupting and reputational risks.

1) Policy and legal risks

EU and national government policies are set to become stricter and stricter, with repercussions that are sure to increase the cost of doing business. These policies may include an obligation to address climate measures and climate risks in yearly reports, further increases of the carbon-emissions tax, stricter regulations on the production and sale of products and services, and further regulations on the climate claims that companies can make in advertising campaigns.

2) Technological risks

Companies are expected to invest in technology to ensure that they can successfully implement their net-zero plan by 2050. This affects all aspects of the life cycle of products and services. Whether it's to do with production, the choice of raw materials, transport, infrastructure, energy use or any other aspect of the business, technological solutions will be needed to reduce total emissions. Any use of technology bears the related risks.

3) Market-disrupting risks

We should expect to experience some climate shocks between now and 2050, which will disrupt the market in a myriad of ways. It's difficult to predict exactly what the consequences will be. They could range from a scarcity of raw materials and subsequent price inflation to changes in consumer habits which new and proactive start-ups will capitalise on. One thing's for certain: these climate shocks will have an impact on our wellbeing. Swiss Re published an estimate of the cumulative negative impact on GDP between now and 2050 (see table 2). Taking into account all the plans and commitments that have been announced to date, we will see a loss of nearly 20% globally, 10% in Europe and 8.5% in Belgium by the middle of the century (2048) in the worst-case scenario.[46] Worldwide, this represents a decline in economic production of roughly 23 billion dollars a year as a result of climate change.[47]

TABLE 2

Economic loss impact In % GDP

	Temperature rise scenario, by mid-century			
	Well-below 2°C increase	2.0°C increase	2.6°C increase	3.2°C increase
	Paris target	The likely range of global temperature gains		Severe case
Simulating for economic loss from rising temperatures in % GDP, relative to a world without climate change (0°C)				
World	-4.2%	-11.0%	-13.9%	-18.1%
Europe	-2.8%	-7.7%	-8.0%	-10.5%
Belgium	-2.5%	-6.3%	-6.4%	-8.5%

4) Reputational risks

Companies face the risk of damaging their reputation if the contribution they want to and can make to solving the climate crisis is viewed as not meaningful enough by their various stakeholders. The business sector must make more of an effort to tackle the climate crisis and the pressure is rising. Governments are imposing rules, while investors seek deeper understanding of the climate risks their investments face. Banks are less willing to loan money to companies with high emissions and NGOs are ready and waiting, prepared to take companies to court if they think they can make a solid case. Employees are also becoming more and more critical of the climate measures being taken by their workplace. We know that young talent chooses companies in line with their own values. They wouldn't even consider working for a company that is making the climate problem worse. More experienced employees are also finding it harder and harder to work for a company that does not take the climate seriously. Caroline Dennett, who worked for Shell as an independent safety consultant, is a good example. Her story at Shell began in the wake of the BP Deepwater Horizon disaster. Shell wanted to upgrade its safety protocols and rules in order to prevent a similar disaster. But in May 2022, enough was enough for Dennett. It wasn't the job itself that led her to quit, but the ambiguity around how Shell was tackling the climate. She sent the email submitting her resignation to management and 1,400 employees. She also posted a video about it on LinkedIn. The video is powerful. You see a determined woman looking straight at the camera while she says: "Today I'm quitting because of Shell's double talk on climate. Shell's stated safety ambition is to "do no harm". It's called "Goal Zero" and it sounds honourable, but they are completely failing on it. They know that continued oil-and-gas extraction causes extreme harms to our climate, to our environment and to people. And whatever they say, Shell is simply not winding down on fossil fuels. They're expanding, with new exploration and extraction projects, against the clear warnings from scientists and dismissing the huge risks from climate change. And I just can't be a part of this anymore."[48] A few days later, the video had 16,192 likes, 1,538 comments and was shared 1,699 times. The story made several national and international newspapers and news stations. As a company, you can't just wonder if you'll be able to attract new talent with your climate commitments, you also have to ask whether you can hold onto older talent.

Carbon-intensive companies, the Carbon Majors like Shell, are facing more and more lawsuits which come with the associated risks to their reputations. The number of climate-related legal cases has exploded around the world. According to the Grantham Research Institute on Climate Change and the Environment at the London School of Economics, there are currently more than 2,000 ongoing climate-related cases.[49] One of the reasons for this boom is that governments are taking more and more legal initiatives for the climate transition, which makes it easier for advocates to evaluate a company's actions. There are now standards which allow us to verify net-zero and recycling claims. If a company's commitments or claims don't live up to those standards, they can be brought to justice. Recent research by the London School of Economics and Political Science (LSE) shows that a record number of climate cases were brought against companies in 2021. They didn't just target the Carbon Majors; food and agriculture, mobility, finance and chemical companies were also affected.[50]

AN OPPORTUNITY FOR MARKETERS

Although the sustainability transition presents risks, it also offers opportunities for growth. The more we are confronted with the ramifications of extreme weather events, the greater the opportunities for growth will become. You have to be a marketer to understand this. But how can you unlock the path to growth?

Growth is for companies that are part of the solution

The greater the climate problem becomes and the more climate anxiety spreads, the more consumers will look for solutions – solutions they hope to find in the business sector. More and more consumer research has confirmed that consumers want companies and their brands to take the lead in the climate transition. Our research with professor Gino Verleye from Ghent University shows that Belgian consumers feel the same: more than eight in ten Belgian consumers (83%) want companies to take action. "It is a historically high figure," Verleye says about the result. "Never before have so many consumers asked the business world to solve a social problem." One of the reasons why this number is so high is that the other crucial party is not responding – political leaders. "Only 7% of Belgians think that politicians can solve the climate problem," adds Verleye. "But there's more: more than half of Belgians (54%) are asking businesses to actively help them adapt their lifestyle to the climate crisis." Consumers struggle to understand exactly how much of an impact they can have on the climate issue. Eating less meat, installing a heat pump and driving an electric car are well-known solutions, but not affordable for most people.

What else is there and how can we have the greatest impact? "Demand for more sustainable product choices will only continue to grow," explains Verleye. But what about the Say-Do gap? Is this another example of consumers saying that they want to buy sustainable items but then failing to follow through? Yes, especially once they see the difference in price. Nevertheless, despite the higher price tag, sales of sustainable products are climbing faster than those of regular products. Research by NYU Stern School of Business has shown that sales of sustainable products are growing 5.6 times faster than regular products and that sales of sustainable products are surging ahead in their product category in 90% of cases. Consumers are evidently making more and more climate-friendly choices and opting for companies they see as part of the solution. This perception will be of even greater importance as time goes by. The more we experience the negative effects of extreme weather events, the more climate anxiety grows, the more people will look for solutions and the more important it will be for companies to be part of the solution. Of course, consumers' attention will occasionally wane when they're confronted with phenomena that temporarily demand more attention, such as rising inflation, out-of-control energy prices or an economic crisis. But this is no reason for the business world to slow down or reduce its efforts to be part of the solution.

Being part of the solution is about credibility

"The question is this: Can you help consumers play their part to solve the climate problem in their everyday lives through your products and services?" says Verleye. But doing this isn't enough to make a brand part of the solution. Brands have a historic deficit they need to surmount – the fact that when they talk about sustainability, they're not believed, as shown in figure 3.

FIGURE 3

People who believe companies are genuine when talking about sustainability (%)

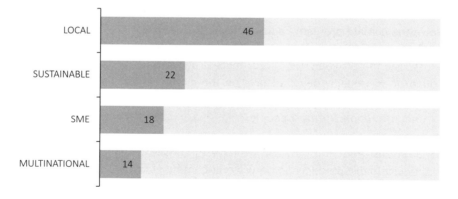

This means that they're also not believed when they present their products as a solution. "Only 14% of Belgian consumers believe multinationals (companies such as Unilever, P&G or Nestle) when they talk about their sustainability efforts. 86% don't. For small and medium-sized enterprises, this increases to 18%. Even companies that position themselves as sustainable only achieve a score of 22%. Local companies score the highest with slightly less than half of consumers thinking they're credible," explains Verleye as he runs through the figures. It's thus understandable that experts deem damage to one's reputation as a transition risk. If you look at the numbers, most consumers think that companies aren't genuine about their climate efforts. The other results of the research support this finding. Although 83% of Belgians want to see businesses take the lead in the climate transition, 81% believe that companies are doing too little. 78% feel the same way about social problems. Being part of the solution thus has everything to do with your credibility. It is your credibility that will ensure that the impact your sustainable products can have is recognised and valued. Without that credibility, any efforts you make will be seen as greenwashing and that's the worst thing a company or brand can be accused of today. Gino Verleye explains: "Belgians are categorical when it comes to greenwashing. If they think that a brand is greenwashing, more than half of Belgians will immediately stop buying from that brand. Growth is there for the taking. The last thing you want is to deny yourself that opportunity because of greenwashing."

If companies want to benefit from climate-friendly opportunities for market growth, they need to be seen as part of the solution in the eyes of the consumer. This isn't easy for several reasons. First of all, few companies start out as part of the solution in the climate normal. The vast majority have to make the transition from a company that isn't climate-friendly to one that is and that takes time and energy. Secondly, every company is starting their race with a credibility disadvantage. There are very few companies that can expect their consumers to believe their climate commitments without any resistance. Everyone else will have to build up their credibility and that also takes time and energy. Of course, companies have no other choice. If they continue to be a part of the problem, they are pushing themselves out of the market in the new climate normal. On the other hand, it's absolutely worth the effort; not only does it open the doors to a burgeoning market for climate-friendly products, it also limits long-term transition risks.

Sustainable needs to become the easy option

Professor Felix Creutzig at the Berlin Institute of Technology, one of the main authors of the latest IPCC report, has also pointed out that consumers are open to companies offering climate-friendly products. He researches the flip side of greenhouse gas emissions, not emissions caused by supply but those caused by demand – in other words, emissions caused by consumers. His research shows that consumers can prevent millions of tonnes of greenhouse gases being emitted. The answer lies in their consumption habits. Until now, climate science has mainly focused on supply, but scientific research on emissions caused by demand has surged since 2014. That's why there's nothing about it in the Paris Agreement, but that all changed with the latest IPCC report. In chapter five, the authors estimated that we could reduce emissions by 40 to 70% by 2050 if consumers resolutely choose sustainable options. That is huge. According to Scientific American, it would be enough to meet the targets of the Paris Agreement, which is great news.[51] Before we thought that the impact consumers could have was limited, but it now seems that they are fundamental to achieving the targets of the Paris Agreement given the current circumstances. It's just a shame that nobody has heard about this possibility. The contents of the latest IPCC report were completely overshadowed by Russia's invasion of Ukraine.

According to Creutzig, we still need hard and soft infrastructure measures to help us achieve this massive reduction among consumers, the kinds of measures that support consumers to adopt a climate-friendly lifestyle. "Today it still feels as if we're swimming against the current," Creutzig explained during our conversation. "The opposite needs to happen: it needs to feel like the easy choice. If we succeed in doing that, we can make a whole lot of progress in a short time."

There are three ways in which we can reduce the emissions generated by consumer habits.

! The first option is an absolute decrease, i.e. reducing the physical quantity of goods and services consumed. Eat less red meat, drive fewer miles, use less energy and so on. Less is better than more. It's the prevailing story line we hear today, but it's not the right one. "Eat less meat!" "Drive less!" "Buy less!" It doesn't sound inspiring and it doesn't encourage. Instead, it makes consumers feel guilty.

! A second option to limit emissions caused by consumer habits is to replace technology that produces high quantities of emissions with lower-emissions alternatives. For example, we can replace a diesel car with an electric car or heat our house with a heat pump rather than gas.

! A third option to reduce consumption is the 'modal shift', in other words stopping any consumption that's not good for the environment. This story is about doing things differently: eat a plant-based diet rather than a diet high in meat, choose only sustainable or second-hand clothing and wear items until they're completely worn out. This story is more inspiring because instead of making do with less, we're doing things differently and that doesn't have to be difficult. It's also inspiring for companies them-selves. Climate-friendly companies are using 'the modal shift' to innovate, which we'll discuss further in the next chapter.

Whatever option you choose, it needs to be combined with hard and soft infrastructure measures. Hard measures include financial incentives that encourage people to choose technological solutions that reduce their emis-sions, such as heat pumps to warm their homes or electric vehicles. Soft measures support the social change needed and include education. In many educational systems, the study of geography is becoming a study of the cli-mate, giving the children of today the information they need for the future. Consumption patterns are an infrastructure element that largely determine the emissions behaviour of consumers. Ensuring that sustainable consump-tion becomes the easy choice and therefore the social norm is an important soft infrastructure measure that can greatly contribute to achieving 70% emissions reductions.

Ensuring that it becomes the social norm? Making it the easy option? Isn't that something that we as marketers and advertising professionals are extremely good at? Chapter 5 of the IPCC report is fantastic news for us because it shows us where we can find potential for growth and how we can unlock that potential. It also demonstrates the positive impact that bol-stering the use of climate-friendly products can have – highly significant emissions cuts. The not so good news is that, like the rest of the report, not many marketers or advertising professionals have heard about this finding, let alone read the report.

More emissions cuts and fewer transition risks

Climate-friendly growth goes hand in hand with more emissions reductions. And that is also an important fact. Companies are not only responsible for the emissions caused by the manufacturing of products but also by the use of their products. Car brands, for example, are responsible for the emissions produced by their cars' combustion engines, not just during production but whenever anyone drives one (this is called scope 3, a topic we'll explore fur-ther in chapter 3). Selling electric cars reduces the total emissions resulting from the use of all their cars. The more companies focus on boosting their climate-friendly products and cutting back on harmful consumption, the better for their own emissions-reduction plans.

But it doesn't stop there. Given that their own policies naturally fit into the new climate normal, climate-friendly companies find it easier to adapt to stricter policy measures and thus limit their transition risks. Moreover, they don't run the risk of damaging their reputation because they don't engage in greenwashing and they're generally not targeted by climate action groups or taken to court, which means that their legal risks are also lower.

FIGURE 4

Climate-friendly growth pathway

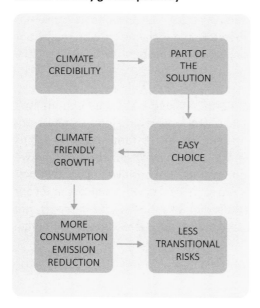

Therefore, the pathway to growth in the new climate normal encompasses a number of factors that companies paid little or no attention to in the old normal. How weak or strong their credibility is with consumers is one of them. But, as we can see in figure 4, credibility is fundamental in the new climate normal. This credibility is key to becoming a company that is seen as part of the solution in the eyes of the consumer. Once one has succeeded on that front, it's about making it as easy as possible for consumers to choose climate-friendly options. That is a company's entry ticket to the fastest-growing market today, which in turn will reduce that company's emissions and limit transition risks.

TIME TO GET CRACKING

The climate crisis is one of the greatest risk mitigation exercises businesses have ever faced in economic history. Ensuring that climate warming stabilises at 1.5 degrees Celsius by the mid-century is the most important mission that humankind has ever had. It is also one of the most complex issues we have ever had to deal with. There are so many dimensions to it – political, social, scientific, psychological, economic and communicative – that it's frankly impossible for one person alone to fully understand it. The problem is also evolving extremely quickly, yet it seems slow at the same time. It's not like COVID-19, where we saw the curve climb exponentially in just two weeks. This crisis gives us the illusion of time. It's also a project with an unseen time-line. After all, the deadline is 2100 when most of us will no longer be alive. In a way, that makes the project unreal and difficult to believe. Is humankind in danger? And by our own doing no less? Our brains are programmed not to believe that. That's why we question it.

The same goes for businesses. We all have a little Stuart Kirk in us saying 'it won't be as bad as they say, and if it gets bad we can solve it'. As a result, we minimise the lack of action to a certain extent. We also all have a little Caroline Dennett in us saying 'enough is enough, it's time for action, we need to take responsibility even if it has its disadvantages'. For the moment, the Stuarts are winning out over the Carolines and will continue to do so as long as we believe that the answer to the climate crisis is a risk mitigation exercise for companies. In risk mitigation, there are always different scenarios with one that doesn't look that bad. Our brains see that option as the most plausible which, in turn, leads to a massive Say-Do gap, even in the business sector.

Nevertheless, the latest IPCC report showed us that the climate crisis isn't just about risk mitigation, it also represents massive opportunities for growth. Felix Creutzig showed us that we can unlock that growth potential if we make sustainable consumption the easy choice and thus make the sustainable choice the social norm. In so doing, that potential for growth comes with an opportunity to considerably reduce emissions. If all conditions are met, sustainable consumption could even lead to a global reduction of 70% in emissions. Some see this as our second chance to achieve the targets of the Paris Agreement. That would be growth with an incredibly positive impact, including for the company itself; by having a larger positive impact, companies run a lower transition risk. The more we see it that way, the more the Carolines will win out over the Stuarts.

Which companies benefit the most from unlocking that potential for growth depends on their climate credibility. Gino Verleye showed that it's not simply a question of bringing climate-friendly products to market and making them the easy choice. First and foremost, it's about being credible enough to be seen as part of the solution. Only if that condition is met can products be valued as they should. Only then can that growth be unlocked. For marketers, this shouldn't be an insurmountable task. On the contrary, that's what marketing is about. It also clearly shows us the role that marketing can play in achieving the goals of the Paris Agreement. Before the latest IPCC report, we didn't really know what we could do to make a difference, but now we have a number that shows exactly what could happen if we start taking responsibility.

In chapter 3, we will look at a number of companies that are proactively seeking climate-friendly growth. We'll delve into what they're doing, analyse a few examples of how they are trying to make climate-friendly consumption the social norm and how their actions align completely with the latest climate insights from the scientific community. In the last chapter, we will focus on how a brand can build the credibility it needs to be seen as part of the solution and thus how to ensure the brand benefits from that growth. We've already seen that consumers are expecting businesses to take the lead on the climate, which means that staying silent is no longer an option. We will delve into the results of Gino Verleye's scientific research which examines how companies communicate today. At the same time, his credibility model will give companies the guidance they need to learn how to speak more confidently and how to say clear and loud that their company is leading the fight for the climate.

Communication and marketing departments must adopt the same mindset as businesses and politicians should when tackling the climate problem: unite behind the science.

THE GREAT HESITATION IN NUMBERS (2)

Extreme weather events today (+1.1°C warming)

(January 2021 – April 2022)[52]

Apr-22	Global	**Fifth-highest** April average global surface temperature on record, tied with 2010
Apr-22	Global	Above average cyclone activity, with 5 named storms
Apr-22	North America	Dry, warm and windy conditions contributed to wildfires across the southwest
Apr-22	South America	Several heavy-rain events occurred throughout the month in Colombia, triggering devastating landslides and dangerous floods
Apr-22	Africa	**Record-breaking** rain fell across parts of South Africa, producing floods that destroyed homes, bridges and roads
Apr-22	Asia	**Warmest** April on record for the continent. Unusually high temperatures affected India and Pakistan at the end of the month, with several locations setting new records
Apr-22	Asia	Tropical Storm Megi brought strong winds and heavy rain to parts of the Philippines, which triggered deadly landslides
Apr-22	Oceania	Several locations in New Zealand had their **driest** April on record
Apr-22	Antarctica	Antarctica sea ice extent for April was 15% below average, and the **fourth-smallest** on record, tied with 1981

Mar-22	Global	**Fifth-highest** March average global surface temperature on record
Mar-22	Global	Above average cyclone activity, with 9 named storms
Mar-22	North America	Several severe weather outbreaks produced strong and damaging tornadoes
Mar-22	Africa	Cyclone Gombe made landfall in Mozambique, bringing devastating winds and heavy rain
Mar-22	Europe	Spain had over twice its normal March precipitation
Mar-22	Asia	Record-warm March temperatures across much of southern Asia
Mar-22	Oceania	Australia had its **fifth-warmest** March on record
Mar-22	Antarctica	Several locations set new March temperature records
Mar-22	Antarctica	Antarctica sea ice extent for March was 30% below average, and the **second-smallest** on record, behind 2017
Feb-22	Global	Above average cyclone activity, with 8 named storms. The South Indian Ocean was the most active basin, with 5 named storms
Feb-22	North America	Heavy rain in northern Puerto Rico at the start of the month triggered dangerous floods and landslides

Feb-22	South America	Torrential rain fell in the city of Petropolis, Brazil, causing deadly flash floods
Feb-22	Europe	Spain had its **third-driest** February since 1961
Feb-22	Asia	Cyclone Emnati made landfall in Madagascar a few days after Cyclone Batsirai and Tropical Storm Dumako. This was the first time since 1988 that 3 storms made landfall in the country in a single month
Feb-22	Oceania	Part of Queensland, Australia, had heavy rain which caused extreme flooding
Feb-22	Antarctica	Antarctica sea ice extent for February was 30% below average, and the **smallest** on record
Jan-22	South America	Much warmer than average temperatures, marking the **second-warmest** January on record behind 2016
Jan-22	South America	Intense heatwave in Argentina
Jan-22	Africa	Cyclone Batsirai was the strongest cyclone to form in January. It made landfall in Madagascar in early February
Jan-22	Asia	**Fourth-warmest** January on record
Jan-22	Oceania	Temperatures higher than 50°C recorded in parts of Western Australia. A maximum temperature of 50.7°C recorded at the Onslow Airport, tying for the nation's **highest** temperature on record

Jan-22	Antarctica	Antarctica sea ice extent for January was 23% below average, and the **second-smallest** on record, behind 2017
Dec-21	Global	Tied with 2016 as the **fifth-highest** December average global surface temperature on record
Dec-21	South America	**Third-warmest** December on record, after 2013 and 2015
Dec-21	Europe	A minimum temperature of-43.8°C was recorded on December 6 in Lapland, marking Sweden's coldest December night in 35 years
Dec-21	Asia	Typhoon Rai makes landfall in the Philippines, wreaking havoc across the region
Dec-21	Antarctica	Antarctica sea ice extent for December was 12% below average, and the **third-smallest** on record
Nov-21	Global	**Fourth-highest** November average global surface temperature on record
Nov-21	Global	21 named storms in the 2021 North Atlantic hurricane season – the **third-highest** number for the season on record
Nov-21	Africa	**Second-warmest** November on record
Nov-21	Oceania	Coolest November since 1999. Australia experiences its wettest November on record, New Zealand has its warmest November on record

Nov-21	Antarctica	Antarctica sea ice extent for November was 6% below average, and the **second-smallest** on record. Only 2016 had a smaller extent
Oct-21	Global	**Fourth-highest** October average global surface temperature on record
Oct-21	North America	**Third-highest** number of named storms on record, 21, during North America›s hurricane season. **Second-warmest** October on record, only 1963 was warmer. **Record rainfall** in parts of California
Oct-21	South America	**Third-warmest** October on record, behind 2014 and 2020
Oct-21	Antarctica	**Fourth-smallest** October sea ice extent on record
Sept-21	Global	**Fifth-highest** September average global surface temperature on record. 75 named storms formed between January and September, the **fifth-most** named storms on record for the period
Sept-21	North America	**Third-warmest** September on record for the continent and **fifth-warmest** on record for mainland USA, which was also hit by Hurricane Nicholas
Sept-21	South America	**Warmest** September on record for the continent, Brazil suffers its worst drought for centuries
Sept-21	Africa	**Warmest** September on record

Sept-21	Asia	Typhoon Chanthu makes landfall in the northern Philippines on September 11, causing widespread damage
Aug-21	North America	Mexico set a new national August **maximum temperature** record, 50.4°C. Significant damage caused to parts of the USA and Cuba by Hurricane Ida
Aug-21	Africa	**Third-warmest** August on record
Aug-21	Europe	**Highest** maximum temperature believed ever to be recorded on the continent: 48.8°C in Sicily, Italy (pending confirmation)
Aug-21	Asia	**Second-warmest** June to August period on record
Aug-21	Antarctica	**Fifth-largest** August sea-ice coverage on record
Jul-21	Global	**Highest** July average global surface temperature on record
Jul-21	Arctic	**Fourth-smallest** July sea-ice coverage on record
Jul-21	Europe	Heatwave in southern Europe with temperatures above 40°C. The continent has its **second-warmest** July on record, tied with 2010 and behind 2018
Jul-21	Asia	**Warmest** July on record. Nine of the 10 warmest Julys in Asia have occurred since 2005
Jul-21	Oceania	**Fourth-warmest** July in Australia on record

Jun-21	Global	**Fifth-highest** average global surface temperature for June on record
Jun-21	Northern Hemisphere	Four named storms through June, tying with 2012, 2016 and 2020 for the **most named storms** so far in the Atlantic hurricane season
Jun-21	North America	**Warmest** June on record for the continent and for mainland USA. Unprecedented heatwave across the north-western US and western Canada
Jun-21	Africa	**Warmest** June on record
Jun-21	Europe	**Second-warmest** June on record
Jun-21	Asia	**Second-hottest** June on record, tied with 2010
Jun-21	Oceania	**Warmest** June in New Zealand on record
May-21	Northern Hemisphere	Seventh consecutive year in which a named storm, Storm Ana, forms before the official start of the Atlantic hurricane season on June 1
May-21	North America	Drought emergencies declared across parts of the western US, torrential rain and flash floods across parts of the Gulf Coast
May-21	Asia	**Second-warmest** May on record, behind 2020. Hong Kong experiences its **warmest-ever** May
Apr-21	North America	**Record snow** for the season across parts of the Ohio Valley and North-eastern US

Apr-21	Africa	**Fourth-warmest** April on record
Apr-21	Europe	Coldest April since 2003
Apr-21	Asia	Typhoon Surigae: **strongest maximum wind speed** ever recorded for a storm during the months of January to April anywhere in the world. Historic floods and landslides in Indonesia following Cyclone Seroja
Apr-21	Oceania	Cyclone Seroja also brings **record-breaking** daily rainfall to several locations in Western Australia. **Fourth-warmest** April on record for New Zealand
Mar-21	Oceania	Widespread damage in New Caledonia, islands in the South Pacific, caused by Cyclone Niran
Jan-21	North America	**Second-warmest** January on record
Jan-21	Africa	**Warmest** January on record, beating the previous high recorded in 2010
Jan-21	Europe	Wetter than average conditions across much of Europe, heaviest March snowfall in Madrid since 1971
Jan-21	Asia	Deadly floods in Malaysia following torrential rain

Unite Behind the Science.

" Every disaster movie begins
with a scientist being ignored.
Neil deGrasse Tyson
Astrophysicist

THE CLIMATE AND BIODIVERSITY ARE
TOP PRIORITIES

Damian Cave, bureau chief of the New York Times in Australia, was queuing in a coffee shop one day. After ordering a flat white, instead of a "Thank you, can I have your name please?" the barista asked him in a slightly reproachful tone: "Don't you have a KeepCup?" He didn't understand what she meant, until he looked around at the other customers in the coffee shop. Everyone had a reusable coffee cup, of some shape and size. Of course, Damian could still order a coffee in one of the shop's non-reusable carton or plastic cups, but it was obviously no longer socially acceptable to do that.[53]

This is a good example of making something the social norm. KeepCup is not the result of a government campaign or NGO actions. The KeepCup company initiated this change. KeepCup is a B corporation founded in 2009 by brother and sister Jamie and Abigail Forsyth. They ran a coffee shop chain in Melbourne and were wholeheartedly concerned when they saw how much waste the disposable, non-recyclable coffee cups were creating (in Australia,

2.7 million cups are thrown away every day). They believed in a reusable alternative, but knew that two fundamental conditions must be met for their idea to have a chance of succeeding. First, the product needed to be approved by baristas. It couldn't make their job more difficult, for example by requiring them to pour coffee from their own cups into a customer's reusable cup. The cup thus had to fit under the nozzles of various industrial coffee machines and correspond to the various sizes of drink on offer. Secondly, it had to be an attractive and, crucially, an easy-to-use alternative for consumers, while also making them feel like they were doing something good for the planet.

They were right. Since then, KeepCup has sold 10 million reusable coffee cups in more than 75 countries, representing an annual turnover of 20 million dollars.[54] But more important to them than their business success, they feel that they have succeeded in encouraging consumers to consume in a way that is better for the climate. In Australia, you drink your coffee from a reusable cup. Point blank. Nowadays, KeepCup is no longer the only reusable option, as there are plenty of competitors on the market. However, the founders of KeepCup think that's brilliant news. The more competitors they have, the more consumers are adopting climate-friendly behaviour.

In 2002, Dutch investigative journalist, Teun Van de Keuken, discovered that many chocolate factories don't abide by the Harkin-Engel Protocol, an international agreement adopted in 2001 banning child labour and forced labour in cacao production. Teun decided to take action. In 2005, he filmed himself eating chocolate, which he then used as evidence in a lawsuit he filed with Dutch courts accusing himself of supporting child slavery. He even asked a number of former child slaves to testify against him. However, the court dismissed the case. The large chocolate manufacturers didn't even raise an eyebrow. Not one made an effort to align itself with the Harkin-Engel agreement. As a result, Teun decided to change tack and produce and sell his own slave-free chocolate bars. Twenty years later, Tony Chocolonely's is the perfect example of a sustainable company. It's a B corporation that raises awareness by exposing social injustice in the chocolate industry. Although KeepCup and Tony Chocolonely's focus on different aspects of sustainability, they both make it easy for consumers to make the sustainable choice. They have both contributed to the sustainability transition by operating within the framework of the Sustainable Development Goals.

The Sustainable Development Goals are the plan developed by the United Nations to safely lead us through the sustainability transition. According to the UN, the world will be sustainable once it meets the needs of the present generation without compromising the ability of future generations to meet their own needs. This isn't the case at the moment. The UN has thus listed our most important sustainability challenges: economic inclusion, biodiversity loss, social injustice, geopolitical instability and the multi-faceted consequences of climate change. In total, the UN has identified 17 challenges and set targets accordingly to be achieved by 2030. Although the agreement was approved by all members of the United Nations in 2015, it came about thanks to input from the business and academic sectors and non-profit organisations. It is an important plan for the business sector as it's the only global plan that offers a holistic solution to the difficult times that are to come. We know that our social structure is breaking down, that our planetary systems are under severe pressure and that both will bring about a number of unpleasant social and economic shocks.

Businesses are handling this in different ways. Some companies look at the SDGs from the point of view of the status quo. They examine what they are already doing today to see if it fits with one or more of the goals. They don't look at what they can do better or how they can make progress. Meanwhile, some companies take a more selective approach. They analyse in which areas they can have a positive impact, choosing the corresponding SDGs and setting goals to do better in the future. Others are taking a more holistic approach and starting with an impact analysis; in other words they evaluate each SDG to see where they are having a positive and negative impact. Next, they explore options to nullify their negative impact and maximise their positive impact.

Figure 5 shows the overall picture which clearly shows that the progress that has been made since 2015 varies greatly from goal to goal. A lot of headway is being made on some SDGs (e.g. SDGs 9, 1 and 5), while several others are lagging behind. The decline for SDG 12 (sustainable consumption and production) shows how urgently companies must step up to the plate. Scientists are particularly concerned about the lack of progress on SDG 6 (clean water and sanitation), 13 (climate action), 14 (life below water) and 15 (life on land), which is making them incredibly anxious. Their concern is easily understandable, if we go back in time 12,000 years.

FIGURE 5

Progress on Sustainable Development Goals 2015-2021

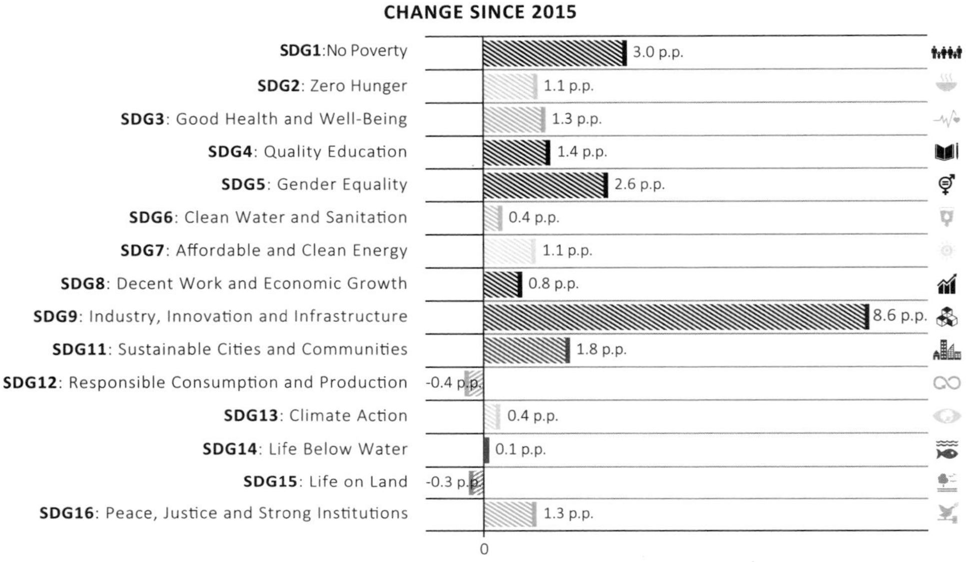

CHANGE SINCE 2015

SDG1:No Poverty	3.0 p.p.
SDG2: Zero Hunger	1.1 p.p.
SDG3: Good Health and Well-Being	1.3 p.p.
SDG4: Quality Education	1.4 p.p.
SDG5: Gender Equality	2.6 p.p.
SDG6: Clean Water and Sanitation	0.4 p.p.
SDG7: Affordable and Clean Energy	1.1 p.p.
SDG8: Decent Work and Economic Growth	0.8 p.p.
SDG9: Industry, Innovation and Infrastructure	8.6 p.p.
SDG11: Sustainable Cities and Communities	1.8 p.p.
SDG12: Responsible Consumption and Production	-0.4 p.p.
SDG13: Climate Action	0.4 p.p.
SDG14: Life Below Water	0.1 p.p.
SDG15: Life on Land	-0.3 p.p.
SDG16: Peace, Justice and Strong Institutions	1.3 p.p.

0

Note: Population-weighted averages. Insufficient data for SDG 10 (Reduced Inequalities) and SDG 17 (Partnerships for the Goals). Time series data for SDG 12 (Responsible Consumption and Protection) is only based on the indicator "Elektronic waste (kg/capita)".

THE HOLOCENE

We are currently living in a time between two glacial periods. Geologically speaking, glacial periods are a normal occurrence and tend to last around 90,000 years. The warmer periods, called 'interglacials', only tend to last a few thousand years before a new glacial period starts. We are currently in an interglacial period that geologists have dubbed the Holocene. It's already lasted nearly 12,000 years, which is abnormally long. Scientists believe that the Holocene could even last up to 50,000 years.[55] This is because of the Earth's current unusual orbit around the sun. The last time an 'interglacial' period lasted longer than normal was around 400,000 years ago. According to geologists, this means we are living in special times. Unfortunately, our impact on the Earth's system is so great that we have singlehandedly brought about the end of this unique epoch.

FIGURE 6

The last 100,000 years temperature change

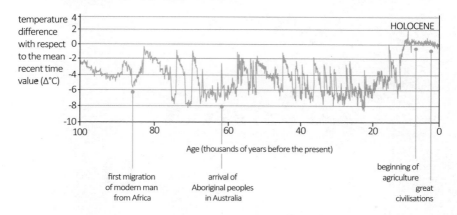

This graph shows the temperature changes on Earth in the last 100,000 years, based on data from the Greenland ice cap. The temperature has been remarkably stable for the last 12,000 years.

The most important characteristic of the Holocene is that it enables a stable climate. The average temperature over the last 12,000 years has fluctuated between plus or minus 2 degrees of warming or cooling. Thanks to this stability, humankind has had the opportunity to develop. We stopped roaming and built settlements, we learned how to farm (with the cultivation of wheat, barley and maize growing rapidly around the world), we tamed sheep, goats, cattle, dogs and cats and lived in harmony with the seasons. The Tundra made way for forests. Mammoths and woolly rhinoceroses, who had adapted to an icy climate for centuries, died out.

We started hunting small game and filling our diet with more and more plants. We saw great civilisations rise, including the Chinese Shang dynasty, the Egyptians, the Maya, the Greeks and the Romans. All in all, the Holocene was good for people. At the beginning of the Holocene, there were a little more than two million people on Earth. In 1000 BC, there were already 188 million of us and this figure will, as we know, continue rising. Climate stability is also the foundation of our economic system, because its predictability has left little room for surprises. It has allowed us to develop our economy, initiate industrial revolutions, invest and innovate with confidence.

OUR FIRST CHANCE TO STABILISE THE CLIMATE AGAIN IS AROUND 2050

In around 1950, we relinquished the stability that made us great and that we now take for granted. We have had such a significant impact on the climate system since then that we're singlehandedly pushing our planet into a new geological period; we closed the door on the Holocene and are entering the Anthropocene – *Anthropos* (Greek for 'person') + suffix *-ceen* (derived from *kainos*, meaning 'new'). As the saying goes: what's done is done. We can't go back to the Holocene. That's not how it works with geological time periods. The instability we're experiencing today will last until at least the middle of this century and will steadily get worse. There's nothing we can do that will regulate the climate crisis before then. Nothing we can do today will bring back climate stability tomorrow; we've emitted too many greenhouse gases for that. Depending on the type of gas, these emissions can remain in the atmosphere for between 10 and 100 years. That's why the business sector is paying so much attention to properly evaluating the climate transition's physical and transition risks. The more unstable the climate becomes, the greater the risks will be. Those risks are easy to understand thanks to the IPCC's fantastic atlas.

Our first chance to stabilise the climate again would bear its fruits in around 2050, as long as we cut greenhouse gas emissions by 43% by 2030, reduce methane emissions by a third and achieve net-zero emissions by 2050. This would allow the climate to stabilise at 1.5 degrees. If we don't manage that, we have a second chance for stabilisation by 2070 but that would mean stabilising the climate at plus 2 degrees. In order for that to work, global greenhouse gas emissions must peak by 2025 at the latest, and be reduced by a quarter by 2030 and CO_2 emissions must reach net-zero by 2070.[56] If we fail to do this, we may as well star in a disaster movie, featuring Earth systems that are out-of-control and humankind as the protagonist.

It's understandable that scientists are worried about the lack of progress on SDG 13: climate action. But the reason why are they concerned about the lack of action on SDG 5 (clean water and sanitation), 14 (life under water) and 15 (life on land) has to do with our planetary boundaries.

THE PLANETARY BOUNDARIES

Even though we can't go back to the Holocene, we still need to make sure that we maintain our planet as close as possible to a Holocene-like, interglacial state. To do this, it is crucial that we keep global warming in check but there are other important factors too. The balance between various Earth systems determines whether our planet remains hospitable for humankind and to what extent. Every Earth system has a critical boundary. If we place too much pressure on one Earth system, we may push it beyond the critical edge. That, in turn, weakens the stability of the whole Earth system. Every system process has a tipping point and if we push it past that point, it will break. To put it in non-scientific terms: if the system breaks, all hell breaks loose. We must thus ensure that any pressure on the Earth's systems remains within those critical boundaries.

The danger lies in the feedback processes. If an Earth system passes its tipping point, it triggers feedback processes that we, as human beings, cannot stop. One such example is the melting of the ice caps in Antarctica. Ice reflects an enormous amount of sunlight and sends it back into space, thus slowing warming. If the ice caps melt, more land mass will be uncovered. Land, contrary to ice, absorbs the sun's rays and contributes to warming. The more ice melts, the more land becomes visible, causing more ice to melt and more land to become visible. At some point, there is no turning back.

Scientists have identified nine important Earth systems and have been able to determine the boundaries of each one. These boundaries define our **Safe Operating Space**, the safe space within which we can safely continue to develop and grow our economy and society. By respecting these boundaries, our planet will remain in a state that benefits from two ice caps and a stable sea level, with forests and marshes that absorb carbon, a climate that reliably supports agriculture and ocean currents that spread warmth predictably. That's exactly what we need.[57] If we put the system under too much pressure, it will start to crack. Too many cracks will undermine the system and instigate the feedback processes. It is thus crucial that we respect the safe space and fit our social and economic activities neatly into it. Respecting our Safe Operating Space is the most important task at hand for humankind, even more important than tackling global pandemics, wars and economic crises. We have nine Earth systems, each with their own boundaries. Are we respecting those boundaries or testing them to their limit? Let's have a look.

1. The climate

The safe limit for our climate is a CO_2 concentration of 350 PPM (parts per million). We surpassed that number a long time ago (see figure 7). Today we have reached 418 PPM, a figure that continues to rise every single day. According to climate scientists, we are precariously close to several tipping points. In March 2022, both of our poles experienced a heatwave unlike any ever recorded; in the South Pole, maximum temperatures were 40°C higher than normal, while in the North Pole they were 30°C higher than normal. As a result of these temperatures, the ice is melting more rapidly and permafrost regions are also thawing quickly.[58] In addition, in March 2022, scientists discovered that the Amazon rainforest was heading for a tipping point of its own.[59] The largest rainforest in the world is losing too much of its capacity to recover from the damage caused by drought, fires and deforestation. All in all, we are clearly not respecting the climate boundary.

FIGURE 7

Monthly mean carbon dioxide emissions

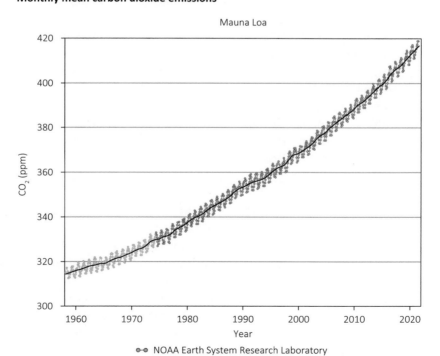

2. Biodiversity

'Living' nature – all the microbes, plants, trees and animals both on land and under water – is crucial to support the stability of our planet. Biodiversity loss on Earth has soared to dramatically high levels and is the result of human activities and the subsequent climate change, pollution and loss of habitat. According to the WWF, 60% of mammal, bird, fish and reptile populations (that have been researched by them) have gone extinct since 1970.[60] One million animals and plants are now threatened with extinction. It is estimated that the extinction of various life forms is now happening 100 times faster than in times before humans and it's picking up speed.[61] The safe boundary for biodiversity is ten species going extinct per million per year. We're well beyond that.

3. Fertiliser (changes in biogeochemical cycles)

In addition to water and sunlight, crops need nitrogen, phosphorus and potassium to grow. Nitrogen and phosphorus, along with other essential nutrients, are contained in the fertilisers we use. The production and use of fertiliser is responsible for 2.4% of global greenhouse gas emissions and more than 20% of total agricultural emissions. That's more than the aviation industry.[62] Furthermore, a significant quantity of the nitrogen and phosphorus contained in fertiliser ends up in the ocean, thus endangering marine life. The safe boundary for the use of phosphorus as a fertiliser is measured by its use, a maximum of 62 million tonnes per year. We currently use 14 million tonnes of phosphorus per year. The same boundary stands for nitrogen, but we've passed it, using 150 million tonnes per year with no slowdown in sight.

4. Deforestation (land system change)

Between 1990 and 2020, approximately 420 million hectares of forest (tropical rainforest in particular) were lost. Every year, another 10 million hectares disappears, an area as big as Scotland and Wales combined.[63] Since we started settling, we've converted too many forests, marshes and grasslands into agricultural land to feed the world population. This has an impact on CO_2 concentrations, waterways, biodiversity and ecosystems, which is why it is crucial for us to reforest. How much forest we need is calculated as a percentage of the forest cover that existed before humans intervened. The safe boundary is a minimum of 75%. We're currently at 62% and falling.

5. Fresh water

Fresh water is the biosphere's blood supply. Neither we, nor the planet, can go without. Research shows that by 2050, nearly half a billion people will face fresh water shortages. The safe boundary for the consumption of blue water (fresh water from streams, rivers and lakes) is a maximum of 4000 km³ per year. We are currently consuming 2600 km³ but that number is climbing. We've already passed the boundary for green-water use, which includes rainwater and soil moisture.

FIGURE 8

Breaking the planetary boundaries

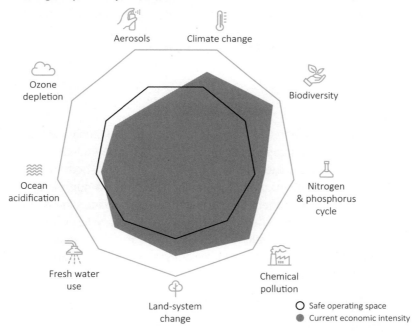

Aerosols Climate change

Ozone depletion

Biodiversity

Ocean acidification

Nitrogen & phosphorus cycle

Fresh water use

Chemical pollution

Land-system change

○ Safe operating space
● Current economic intensity

6. Oceans

Oceans cover 70% of our planet. Rockström calls them our planet's engine room, because they regulate the heat exchange between the Earth's surface and the atmosphere, the water cycle and the distribution of essential nutrients. They store 93% of the heat that we have caused by burning fossil fuels. If they didn't store that heat, we wouldn't be facing warming of more than 1 degree today, but warming of more than 27 degrees.

Our CO_2 emissions have caused the oceans to become 26% more acidic since the industrial revolution. Combined with pollution and rising water temperatures, one of the consequences is that the Great Barrier Reef is dying. At the moment, the level of acidification is still within safe boundaries.

7. Chemical pollution

Today we know of approximately 350,000 different types of manufactured chemicals. These include pesticides, antibiotics, plastic and industrial chemicals. Once they're in the biosphere, they hang around for a very long time. They're known as 'forever chemicals' or PFAS (poly-fluorinated alkyl substances). We have learned that if they make it into the food chain and build up in the tissue of animals and people, they may affect fertility and pose a risk of permanent genetic damage. In January 2022, a number of scientists concluded that we have passed the planetary boundary for chemical pollution.

8. Air pollution

Everyone has seen those smoggy pictures of cities in China and India. That smog contains microparticles of aerosols that have ended up in the air in the form of smoke, dust and polluting gases. In addition to causing the deaths of millions of people per year, it's having a number of adverse effects on the biosphere. Those microparticles create clouds that cool and warm the Earth outside of the normal natural cycles, thus having an impact on rainfall and altering how sun rays are reflected and absorbed around the particles. Scientists have not yet succeeded in determining this planetary boundary.

9. The ozone layer

We already discussed this topic in chapter one. Scientists expect that the hole will be completely closed by 2060.

FIGURE 9

Planetary bounderies and global collapse risk scenarios

HIGH-RISK WORLD

EARTH UNDER UNCERTAINTY

Planetary boundaries have not been extensively crossed

High risk of GCR events

GCR events have potentially occurred/are occurring

Global targets are in danger

GLOBAL COLLAPSE

Planetary boundaries have been extensively crossed

High risk of GCR events

GCR events have potentially occurred/are occurring

Global targets have not been achieved

STABLE EARTH

Planetary boundaries have not been extensively crossed

Successful policy implementation

Low risk of GCR events

Need for implementation of preventative policy

EARTH UNDER THREAT

Planetary boundaries have been extensively crossed

Low risk of GCR events; however, increasing due to planetary boundaries being crossed

Global target achievement in danger

WITHIN LIMITS

THE TIP

LOW RISK WORLD

Note: GCR = global collapse risk.
Source: Cernev (2022)

We have pushed six of the nine regulators of our Earth system beyond their safe limits: climate change, biodiversity loss, deforestation, fertiliser use, fresh green-water use and chemical pollution. It's thus understandable that scientists are getting anxious about the lack of progress being made on SDG 13 (climate action), SDG 6 (clean water and sanitation), SDG 14 (life under water) and SDG 15 (life on land). These four SDGs are the planetary SDGs, which aim to respect the planetary boundaries. If we fail to make steps in the right direction, we will be degrading our own 'Safe Operating Space'. As a consequence, our planet will continue to move away from the safe,

Holocene-like state we have enjoyed. That's not just bad news, it's a point from which we can't turn back. Sometimes it's fun to walk the untrodden path. In this case, it is definitely not, according to the latest report from the United Nations Office for Disaster Risk Reduction. I struggled to breathe when I read their predictions about the risks that we are facing as a society. This is not a club of doomsayers or supporters of the Deep Adaptation movement or advocates of *degrowth* thinking. This is scientific work by the UN. In the report, they explore four risk scenarios. On the one hand, they examine 'Global Cata- strophic Risk' (GCR) which is defined as the risk of a catastrophe affecting an area larger than the hemisphere in which it starts, killing millions of people and causing economic loss of trillions of dollars. In other words, it's the risk of complete social and economic collapse. On the other hand, the report exam- ines what would happen if we achieve or fail to achieve the SDGs. The analysis is based on four scenarios: a world with high or low global catastrophe risk where the planetary boundaries have been crossed or not.

The four resulting potential scenarios are: Earth Under Uncertainty, Global Collapse, Stable Earth and Earth Under Threat. In all four scenarios, with the exception of Stable Earth, the achievement of the SDGs is threatened and the planetary boundaries are exceeded. The conclusion of the report is that "the scenarios show a dangerous tendency for the world to move towards a global collapse scenario. In the absence of change, scenarios Earth Under Uncertainty and Earth Under Threat tend towards that of Global Collapse."[64] In other words, if we fail to achieve the targets set out in the SDGs and don't manage to relieve the strain on the Earth systems, we will enter an unprece- dented danger zone that in all likelihood will lead to social collapse.

Tom Cernev is a researcher at the University of Cambridge and the man behind the four scenarios. I asked him where we stand at the moment. His answer can be summed up in just two words: not good. He confirmed that we've fallen so far behind on working towards the achievement of the SDGs that our chances of reaching those targets by 2030, as was initially decided in 2015, are zero. I asked him if there is a timeline for the four scenarios or an estimate of when global collapse could occur, but there are no estimates yet because a number of determining factors must still be established. First, there's technological development, a chance that we will invent a ground-breaking technology, to help us achieve our climate and biodiversity goals, that can be rolled out quickly and widely enough. But the closer we get to 2050, the fewer chances we have to ensure that any such solution could be implemented on time.

A second factor is the geopolitical situation. In 2015, when the Paris Agreement was signed, there was very strong consensus among the various parties. In Glasgow last year, it was obvious that this consensus had taken a hard beating. Eight months later, in June 2022 at the climate summit in Bonn, it was clear that the commitments made in Glasgow were being put under severe strain by the current inflation and energy crisis and the war in Ukraine. The third factor is the potential timeframe of the effects of climate change on the various Earth systems. The knowledge that we have gained about the planetary boundaries is very new. How the Earth's different systems will react to their boundaries being passed is something we don't yet fully understand. We may thus experience repercussions in one or two decades that we cannot yet predict.

The last factor is the 'unknown unknowns'. These are factors that have an impact on the evolution of the climate crisis but that we don't yet know anything about, not even their existence. Consequently, we also don't know how important or unimportant they are. These four factors make it very difficult to establish a timeline for any of the four scenarios but that doesn't mean that these predicted scenarios aren't realistic. "In short, it is too difficult to predict collapse, but the direction in which humanity is going is extremely concerning and we need to take action as soon as possible," concluded Cernev during our conversation. In short, we can now understand why scientists are getting so anxious about the lack of progress made on SDG 6 (clean water and sanitation), 13 (climate action), 14 (life under water) and 15 (life on land).

The evidence is clear; we need to direct more attention at the four planetary SDGs so that we can stabilise the climate and stop biodiversity loss. Of the nine planetary boundaries, these two present the highest risk if they pass their tipping points. In contrast with the other systems, climate and biodiversity are important enough that they determine how difficult it becomes to survive on Earth. That's why they are the top priorities for the UN and why there is also a Paris Agreement for biodiversity. The Post-2020 Global Biodiversity Framework includes 21 targets and ten milestones that countries agreed must be achieved by the end of the decade.

The climate and biodiversity crises must also be the top two priorities for the business sector. If there's any doubt as to how far-reaching the consequences of passing the climate and biodiversity boundaries would be for our economy, here are two examples. Let us begin with the climate crisis. Of course, we know about the impact on temperatures, but there are also many side effects. François Gemenne, one of the authors of the IPCC report, explained: "We must consider that climate change is really a matrix of risks and that all the issues that will be key in the 21st Century—with development, security, migration, health—all of these issues will be transformed by climate change."[65] A good example of this complexity is the permafrost. Changes in the permafrost, the land in the North that has been frozen for centuries, are one of the tipping points that climate scientists are keeping an eye on. This is because there are enormous quantities of methane and nitrous oxide, two greenhouse gases, trapped in the permafrost. The more the permafrost thaws, and it already is thawing, the more methane and nitrous oxide are released. If we reach that tipping point, the resulting feedback effect would drive climate change even more rapidly: higher temperatures thaw the permafrost faster, methane and nitrous oxide are released, the temperature rises even more as a result.

The thawing of the permafrost is thus a climate issue. But what does that mean for Russia, for example? Permafrost covers 60% of the total landmass of Russia. The thawing of the permafrost is thus dangerous for many cities, buildings and (gas, oil and military) infrastructure that are built on it. It's expected that the capacity of the permafrost to support buildings will fall by a third by 2050, which represents an inherent infrastructure risk of a value of 132 billion dollars.[66] Consequently, the thawing of the permafrost is not just a dangerous tipping point for climate change, but also a danger to the infrastructure built on it and the people living on it. But that's not all. The fossil-fuel industry represents 15 to 20% of Russia's annual GDP.[67] Today some sites have already become unusable due to the thawing permafrost, and many more will become unusable if it continues. It's thus also a growing economic problem.

Biodiversity also plays a key role. We don't pay for the raw materials that the Earth produces, but they have massive economic value. Biodiversity generates more than 150 billion dollars in economic value every year, twice the global GDP, in the form of food supply, carbon storage and water-and-air filtration. Biodiversity loss is already costing the global economy more than 5 billion dollars a year.[68] However, the risks are far greater. According to the WEF, half of our global GDP is highly dependent on well-functioning natural ecosystems but they are becoming weaker and weaker. Today we are well aware which industries are putting so much strain on biodiversity, as five large sectors are responsible for 90% of the damage: food, mobility, energy, fast-fashion and the combination of pharmaceutics and cosmetics.

FIGURE 10

The SDGs Wedding Cake by Johan Rockström

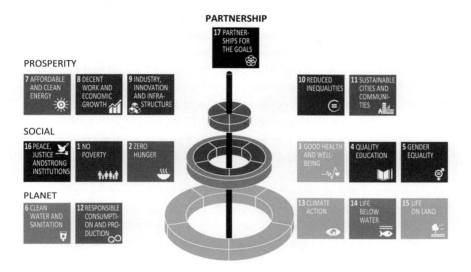

In order to ensure that everyone understands how important the planetary SDGs are, Johan Rockström created a visual aid, now known as the 'SDGs Wedding Cake', that displays the mutual relationships between them. As shown in figure 10, the bottom layer is composed of the planetary SDGs (climate and biodiversity). Above that are the social SDGs which focus on poverty, hunger, education, health, equality, and peace and justice. The top layer contains the SDGs that aim to ensure our economic growth. Finally, SDG 17 is the cherry on the cake, proof that we can achieve all of the SDGs if we work together. The 'wedding cake' clearly shows that social and economic SDGs are only achievable if we build them on top of the planetary SDGs. In other words, if we don't deliver on the planetary SDGs, it will be very difficult to achieve any of the others. In *The Decade of Action*, Rockström explains the importance of the planetary SDGs: "These are non-negotiable. These are the planetary SDGs that everyone simply has to accept."[69] To put it simply, everyone has to work toward hitting these goals, even the business sector. When I shared this statement with Felix Creutzig, he fully supported it. In his opinion, the climate and biodiversity must be the two top priorities for business, because that's where the greatest danger of economic instability lies. Peter Kalmus, climate scientist at NASA, says: "Our economic system is embedded in the biosphere. If we take down the biosphere, we lose everything, and we don't have an economic system anymore."[70] In other words, we need to act swiftly to ensure that we respect the boundaries of both Earth systems. We have seen what the risks are if we don't. Nevertheless, it will only be possible if the business sector stands firmly behind this purpose by making these two concerns their absolute priority. Every company must explore how quickly it can reduce its negative impact on the four planetary SDGs and increase the positive impact. The planetary SDGs should thus be an integral part of any business plan. It's about uniting behind the science. Any company that has selectively chosen which SDGs to tackle must ensure that they have included the planet and, if they haven't, make it a priority. Companies that have taken a holistic view must also prioritise the planetary SDGs. But doesn't that just make things more complex and difficult for businesses? Is it economically feasible? Let us start with that first question.

Imagine a couple at a table in a restaurant. On the front of the menu, you can make out the name of the restaurant – *Meat Out* – so it must be a meat restaurant. The woman asks the man if he's already decided what to order. Not yet. He's tempted by the *Hell of a Steak*, but there is no description of it. He asks the server if he can tell him a bit more about it, which delights the server. "I'm glad you asked. You won't believe what we go through just to bring it to your plate!" He sums it up: "We take a piece of land about the size of three football fields. We water it with more than 3 million litres of water to produce more than 8000 kg of feed and hay to feed a single cow. All of that just to serve you a *Hell of a Steak*. And don't get me started on the greenhouse gases." The couple look bewildered, struggling to take in so many new facts in a very short amount of time. The man responds: "I don't want to know the price." "I'm sure you don't," says the server, "it's a heavy price to pay." Then, a sentence appears on the screen: "A plant-based diet is the single biggest way to reduce your environmental impact and fight global warming." This TV advert was first shown in May 2022 during the final of the Eurovision song festival in Israel, before being broadcast in the UK and US. The organisation that launched the campaign is Vegan Friendly, a non-profit organisation that wants to draw consumers' attention to the negative impact of meat on the climate and biodiversity. It's a good example of how a communications project can influence both climate- and biodiversity-friendly consumption. It's having a real impact; the video is travelling around the world via social media.

Encouraging consumer behaviour that is good for the climate and biodiversity doesn't have to be complex. The climate and biodiversity are closely linked. Climate change has severe implications for biodiversity loss, while

THE SOCIAL AND ECONOMIC SDGS ARE ONLY ACHIEVABLE IF WE BUILD THEM ON TOP OF THE PLANETARY SDGS

ecosystems are of crucial importance to the climate, including for the capture and storage of excess CO_2 in the ground. For ease, we will refer to both the climate and biodiversity as the 'climate' in this book. When we speak about climate-friendly consumer behaviour, we are thus talking about consumer behaviour that is good for both the climate and biodiversity.

DOES CLIMATE FRIENDLINESS SELL?

The second question was: Is it economically feasible? Many experts were concerned that the global pandemic would slow down the momentum that the climate emergency had garnered among the general public before the pandemic. They couldn't have been more wrong. Widespread lockdowns showed the public a world with less traffic, less noise pollution and fewer emissions. We noticed the birds singing and the grass smelling greener. According to InSites Consulting, 57% of European consumers said that the lockdown made them reflect on nature and the importance of clean air.[71] Two in three Europeans also considered the climate crisis to be as important as the pandemic, which should come as no surprise. Many people believe that the essential policies implemented to quash the pandemic are an indication of what must be done to curb the climate crisis.

FIGURE 11

What keeps Gen Z awake at night?

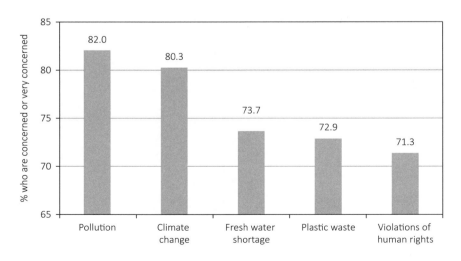

Many Belgians lie awake at night because of climate change and the biodiversity crisis. Younger generations, in particular, are extremely worried. This was evident in the research for the book that I wrote with professor Gino Verleye, *De Duurzame Belg*. Figure 11 shows that the four greatest concerns for Generation Z in Belgium are linked to the climate and biodiversity with pollution (82%) and climate change (80%) topping the list.[72] This is also the case for Millennials, as we can see in figure 12, for whom pollution (83.5%) and climate change (76%) are also leading causes of concern. This is not just how people in Belgium feel. When Europeans were asked what sustainability means to them and what they are most troubled by, most of the concerns people mentioned can be related back to the planetary SDGs. The climate and biodiversity crisis is thus also a key concern for European consumers, as shown in figure 13.[73]

FIGURE 12

What keeps Millennials awake at night?

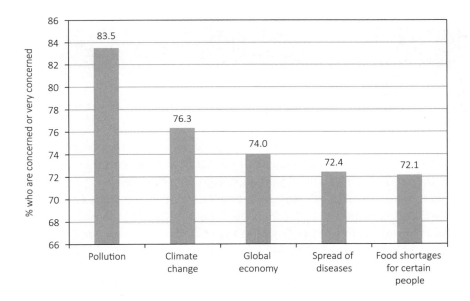

When respondents were asked what the priority should be in terms of sustainability, their answers were all related to the climate and biodiversity. Decreasing CO_2 emissions (53%) came first, followed by recycling (51%), reduced plastic packaging (49%), less food waste (48%) and fair wages and good working conditions (21%). For comparison, decreasing CO_2 emissions was important for 43% of consumers before the pandemic. It seems that the pandemic has had a positive impact on how we see sustainability, with the climate becoming an issue of the utmost importance.

FIGURE 13

Overwhelmingly, European consumers' key concerns are related to the environment

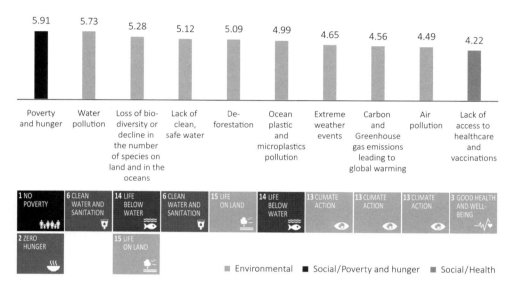

This change is also clearly evidenced by the growth of climate-friendly consumer behaviour: 85% of retailers in the EU have experienced an increase in the sales of climate-friendly products with 65% even reporting a surge of more than 10%, according to a report by the International Trade Centre and the European Commission.[74] Companies expect this growth to continue in the future: nearly all retailers (92%) expect sales of sustainable products to come up in the next five years, with 74% even predicting growth of more than 10%.

For more details, we need to head across the pond. NYU Stern School of Business in the US carries out annual research into the growth of climate-friendly products. They research 250,000 consumer products in 36 categories.[75] All of these products have a thorough climate-friendly product commitment, not products that simply use recyclable packaging or a vague promise like 'made with natural ingredients'. Their latest report showed that climate-friendly products represent a market share of 17%, an increase of 3.3% compared to 2015 with significant growth during the pandemic. Climate-friendly consumption is thus also gaining ground in the US.

TABLE 3

Sustainability priorities for European consumers

1	CO$_2$ reduction	53%
2	Recycling	51%
3	Less plastic	49%
4	Less food waste	48%
5	Fair wages	21%

FIGURE 14

Sustainable products represent less than one-fifth of the market share, but deliver one-third of growth

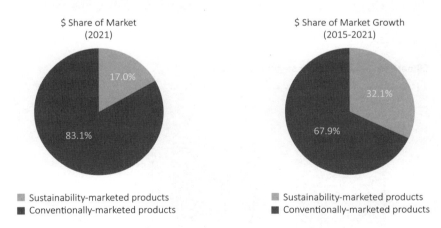

$ Share of Market (2021)

17.0%

83.1%

$ Share of Market Growth (2015-2021)

32.1%

67.9%

▨ Sustainability-marketed products
■ Conventionally-marketed products

Note: Based on 36 categories examined.

Despite the fact that climate-friendly products account for a market share of 17%, which is less than a fifth of the market, they deliver almost a third of growth (32%), as shown in figure 14. Sales of these products are growing 2.7 times faster than those of regular products and twice as fast as the market as a whole. This boom in growth hasn't gone unnoticed by brands, who are responding with new climate-friendly product innovations. Last year, nearly half (48%) of all new products were climate-friendly. This curve hasn't stopped climbing since 2017, when only 28% of new products were climate-friendly. Many of these new products bear a carbon label. Climate-friendly sales doubled in 2021 compared to the previous year and totalled 3.4 billion dollars.

WHO MAKES CLIMATE-FRIENDLY PURCHASES?

Research by Kantar in 2021 shows that we can divide European consumers into four categories, with similar groups in the US.[76] The 'Actives', who represent 31% of consumers in the EU, are very committed to the climate and make a great deal of effort to reduce their impact. They feel an intrinsic responsibility to be more sustainable, actively inform themselves about the topic and are thus able to discuss it at length. They are also prepared to buy products and services from companies that are honestly trying to do good, even if it comes with a higher price tag. The consumption habits of this third of European consumers align with their beliefs; there is no difference between what they do and what they say. In the US, this group represents 33% of the population.

FIGURE 15

Climate friendly consumer segmentation (%)

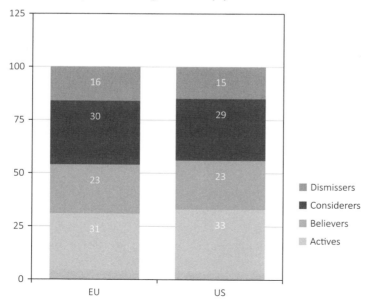

Kantar calls the second group the 'Believers'. Accounting for 23% of consumers (in both the EU and US), they also believe that they can make a difference through the way in which they consume. They're very concerned about the climate but their willingness to act is more limited. They will mostly opt for ease and lower prices, which results in them often not purchasing sustainable products. This is where the barriers start to show. The 'Considerers', the third group, are also very aware of climate and biodiversity issues, but doubt whether their product choices can actually make a difference. They are willing to act, but are limited by their own doubts. This group represents 30% of consumers in the EU and 29% in the US. Finally, the 'Dismissers' represent 15% of consumers in the US and 16% in the EU. We don't need to go into much detail here. They don't attach any importance to the climate, don't know much about it and are not interested in solving it. According to Kantar, the actively climate-friendly group (the Actives) will surge from 31% today to 62% by 2030 in the UK and we assume that the same will happen in the rest of Europe. Subsequently, by 2030, most people will buy products from climate-friendly companies that are part of the solution. Companies that are part of the problem will be left behind and find it harder and harder to sell to consumers.

This research confirms the strategic importance of being climate-friendly: climate-friendly brands will come out on top at the end of the day. Any brands that are now still seen as part of the problem had better do their homework fast to design and implement a climate-friendly business strategy. Some companies will find this more difficult than others. Companies in the aviation, fossil-fuel, fast-fashion and meat-production industries will have their work cut out. It's important for marketers to start asking themselves today how they can build this perception of being good for the climate, because brands cannot become part of the solution overnight. This also deserves much more attention from brands that are already in transition. We have learned that all brands start with a sustainability credibility deficit. It's going to be an uphill climb in order to earn the perception of being one of the good ones.

In Belgium, we have also noticed similar groups of consumers. In our research, we found three groups. We called them the 'Movers', the 'Moveables' and the 'Resisters'. The 'Movers' represent 43% of Belgians and can be compared to the 'Actives'. Their behaviour reflects their values, as long as the barriers to that behaviour are not too high. These are people who talk about the climate crisis and try to convince others to also take action. They prefer local products, monitor their energy use, occasionally buy second-hand and would rather repair items than throw them away. They want to eat a healthier diet, try to eat less meat and buy sustainably. The 'Moveables' are a little less willing to act. For them, the barriers are a bit higher; sustainable items are too expensive and they have considerable doubts about whether their behaviour can actually make a difference. They also lack knowledge of what exactly they can do now. The 'Resisters' are like the 'Dismissers'. They believe it's not their problem. We also expect that 'Movers' will increase in number as more and more people shift over from the Moveable group.

WHAT ABOUT THE CRISIS? WHAT DOES THE FUTURE HOLD?

Now that the coronavirus pandemic is behind us, we can see that the climate-friendly movement has not faltered for even an instant. We can question whether the current geopolitical situation will slow down that growth. It is to be expected that the combination of a war in Europe, the after-effects of the pandemic and an energy crisis, along with the resulting historic inflation rates, may have an impact on climate-friendly consumer behaviour. A drop in purchasing power does not bode well for higher-priced climate-friendly products. It's still too soon to draw any conclusions with any certainty, but research by Kantar in April 2022 seemed to show some interesting activity. First of all, there seems to be little correlation between someone's financial situation and their overall opinion of sustainability. If you're committed to the cause, you will remain committed. Nevertheless, the more precarious your financial situation becomes, the more difficult it will be for you to follow through on that commitment. Climate-friendly consumers don't like that. They believe that companies must now do their bit as well. In other words, companies should make climate-friendly products a bit cheaper so that consumers can continue buying them. They're calling for more of SDG 17 (partnerships for the goals), which is not surprising.

We know that consumers want the business sector to take leadership in the climate-friendly transition. We also know that consumers expect them to do more than they are doing today. First and foremost, this can be achieved by boosting their own positive impact and ensuring that consumers are empowered to make the sustainable choice in store. However, if purchasing power is put under pressure, higher-priced goods will not be a viable option. Consumers are sure they can be made cheaper, because being climate-friendly is not a luxury but a necessity. They thus expect the business sector to help ensure continued progress in the transition so that it is not halted or hindered by painful, but hopefully temporary, problems like higher inflation. Consumers know all too well that the transition won't be a smooth ride. If it were, climate anxiety wouldn't be so high. Consumers also know that the climate crisis will have much more serious ramifications than a war in Europe. That's why it's so important for the transition to pick up the pace rather than slow down, and for the business sector to take responsibility to make sure that happens.

The economic shock we're experiencing today will probably not be the only one between now and 2050. We know that there will be climate shocks, which are sure to hurt the economy too. What is happening now is obviously no blueprint of what will happen in the future, but the dynamics are clear. If times get tough, consumers expect companies to make extra effort to help them continue consuming in a climate-friendly way. We've seen how important it is for companies to tackle their credibility deficit to ensure that they are part of the solution in the eyes of the consumer. This seems like a good opportunity to prove that.

THE MESSAGING FROM SCIENTISTS IS CLEAR

In the village where I grew up, there is an old branch of the river Scheldt. When we had harsh winters, the water froze over and skaters took to the ice. When those first skaters appeared, the local authorities put up a sign warning us: "Skating is prohibited and thus done at your own risk." The message was clear: daredevils who ignored the skating ban and made their way onto the ice would be responsible for paying the bill of any rescue operation.

Similarly, the message coming from scientists today is unambiguous and is being repeated on a daily basis. Still we ignore it, also at our own risk. The more pressure we put on the planetary boundaries, the more unstable the climate and our planet become, the more risks businesses will face. Our economy can only keep growing within the safe space defined by the planetary boundaries. In order to return to that safe space, we need to shift toward a more climate-friendly economy, which will cost a lot of money. Nevertheless, as many experts have estimated, the cost of the alternative – that is to say, continuing with business as normal – will be much higher.

Both consumers and scientists believe that the transition must be led by the business sector. It's also in the best interest of businesses themselves; it's the best way for them to keep a handle on the physical and transition risks. Consumers thus play a dual role. On the one hand, they're asking businesses to provide more solutions, but they're also letting themselves be misled in favour of leaving things as they are. As a result, businesses are questioning when is the right time is to kick things up a gear. On the other hand, consumers represent a prime potential source of emissions cuts, significant enough to fulfil the Paris Agreement according to some estimates. Knowing that all of our current plans and regulations will bring us closer to 3 degrees than 1.5 degrees, and that that would be the difference between a flourishing economy and an economy undergoing a crisis of a scale we cannot predict today, the only reasonable conclusion is that we need to kick things up two gears to overcome the barriers standing in the way of consumers and preventing them from adopting climate-friendly consumption habits. Let us now explore how climate-friendly companies are doing this today.

THE GREAT HESITATION

11 tools to understand the impact of the Great Hesitation

Coastal Risk Screening Tool
An interactive map showing areas threatened by sea level rise and coastal flooding. Combining the most-advanced global models of coastal elevations with the latest projections for future flood levels.

https://coastal.climatecentral.org

IPCC WGI Interactive Atlas
A tool for flexible spatial and temporal analyses of much of the observed and projected climate change information underpinning the Working Group I contribution to the Sixth Assessment Report, including regional synthesis for Climatic Impact-Drivers (CIDs).

https://interactive-atlas.ipcc.ch

The real-time air pollution exposure calculator
The first real-time air pollution exposure calculator, developed by the UN Environment Programme, builds on the world's largest air quality data platform bringing together real-time air pollution data from over 4,000 contributors, including citizens, communities, governments and the private sector to work towards healthier, more sustainable cities.

https://www.iqair.com/air-quality-map

Climate Trace

This coalition of organisations is building a timely, open, and accessible account of exactly where greenhouse gas emissions are coming from. It tracks greenhouse gas (GHG) emissions with unprecedented detail and speed, delivering information that is relevant to parties working to achieve net-zero global emissions.

https://www.climatetrace.org/inventory

The Climate Clock

It melds art, science, technology, and grassroots organisation to get the world to act in time. The Climate Clock is centred on a simple tool: a clock that counts down the critical time window to reach zero emissions while tracking our progress on key solution pathways.

https://climateclock.world

Wikirate.org

WikiRate.org is an open data platform that brings corporate ESG data together in one place, making it accessible, comparable, and free for all.

https://wikirate.org

The Transition Pathway Initiative

The Transition Pathway Initiative (TPI) is a global, asset-owner led initiative which assesses companies' preparedness for the transition to a low carbon economy. It is rapidly becoming the go-to corporate climate action benchmark.

https://www.transitionpathwayinitiative.org/sectors

MSCI Net-Zero Tracker

The MSCI Net-Zero Tracker indicates the collective progress of publicly listed companies in the MSCI ACWI Investable Market Index (IMI) in keeping global warming well below 2°C. It also highlights the largest listed companies with improved climate disclosures, as well as those that lag.

https://www.msci.com/research-and-insights/net-zero-tracker

The Net Zero Tracker

It aims to increase transparency and accountability of net-zero targets pledged by nations, states and regions, cities and companies. The Net Zero Tracker collects data on targets set and on many factors that indicate the integrity of those targets — essentially, how serious the entity setting the target is about meaningfully cutting its net emissions to zero.

https://zerotracker.net

Climate Governance Integrity Programme

Through the Climate Governance Integrity Programme, Transparency International (TI) works to ensure that climate funds are governed with integrity, transparency, and accountability, so that these funds help the most vulnerable people adapt to the climate crisis. Countries receiving climate finance desperately need and deserve it; allowing scarce funds to be stolen is not an option.

https://www.transparency.org/en/projects/climate-governance-integrity-programme

Greenwash.com

Created by the changing markets foundation, it's a non-profit formed to accelerate and scale up solutions to sustainability challenges by leveraging the power of markets.

https://greenwash.com

Breaking down barriers.

> **The economy is a wholly owned subsidiary of the environment, not the reverse.**
> Herman E. Daly
> *American ecologist and economist*

Break down barriers – that is exactly what professor Creutzig expects the business sector to do. Businesses must make climate-friendly options the easy choice and break down any barriers that may stand in the way of consumers choosing those options. The business sector could do something about this tomorrow if they wanted to and would also be in their best interest. The faster the transition, the smaller the transition risks in the short-term and the physical risks in the long run. Barriers exist in various forms, including ease, knowledge and affordability. Companies that are a part of the solution do everything they can to reduce these barriers, but how do they do it?

AFFORDABILITY

Our research showed that, in 2020, 67% of Belgians considered climate-friendly products to be expensive, dropping to 56% in 2021. Kearney's Carsten Gerhardt agrees with consumers. His research showed that climate-friendly products are on average 75% to 85% more expensive than their regular equivalents in Europe.[77] Depending on the product category, this price difference can soar to 220%, as shown in figure 16. There's a similar trend in the US, where climate-friendly products were 27.6% more expensive than regular alternatives in 2022. However, those numbers are falling; the price gap was at 40% in 2018. Differences in price can reach 136%.[78]

Gerhardt believes that these price differences are sabotaging the sustainability transition. He maintains that there is no reason for prices to be so high anymore, arguing that the price could actually be considerably lower if brands and retailers were to make an effort. He estimates that approximately 70% of consumers are happy to pay up to 10% more for a climate-friendly product, 15% would consider paying an additional 30% and the remaining 15% would be prepared to pay an even higher price. A product that is 10% more expensive would thus be widely accepted on the mass market, according to Gerhardt, which would significantly bolster consumption of sustainable products.

FIGURE 16

Price markups for sustainable products

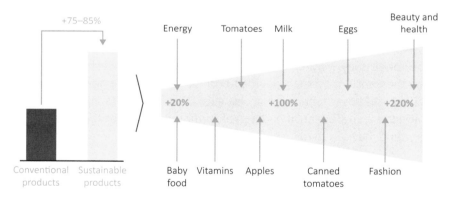

Research by the Boston Consulting Group confirms that sustainable products could be cheaper. They believe that many companies overestimate the cost of decarbonising products. Given how small an impact the cost of raw materials has on the end price of most products, these items should only be 1 to 4% more expensive, even if the whole value chain were completely net-zero. This would vary from a difference in cost of less than 500 euros for a car to less than 0.01 euros for a soft drink (see figure 17).[79]

FIGURE 17

Full decarbonisation has little impact on the end price

Automotive	Fashion	Food	Construction	Electronics	Soft drinks
<€500	<€1	<€1	<€5k	<€3	<€0.01
<2% average cost increase on a €30k car	<2% average cost increase on a €40 pair of jeans	<4% average cost increase on a €20 shopping basket	<3% average cost increase on a €150k home	<1% average cost increase on a €400 smartphone	<1% average cost increase on a €0.90 bottle

Ilke Homes, a British company that builds prefab homes, recently launched Ilke Zero[80]. The aim of this strategy is to build carbon-neutral homes, that amazingly have no monthly energy bills. Ilke calls it building "ZERO carbon, ZERO bills, ZERO cost". Solar panels, battery storage and air-source heat pumps are installed to make the houses energy self-sufficient. Ilke works with energy provider, Octopus, to make sure that the lights don't go out if the solar panels don't produce enough energy. The two companies are working together to trial the scheme in two-bedroom semi-detached family homes in Essex. They plan to expand the project to more than 10,000 homes by 2030. When asked why Ilke is taking this step, CEO Giles Carter said: "The most powerful word in marketing is free. How do we create a carbon transition? We create a proposition that consumers can engage with. If you can offer zero bills and save the planet as well, then you're on the right track."

KNOWLEDGE

Nearly half of Belgians (47%) say that they lack the knowledge they need to adapt their consumption habits properly. They want to, but they don't know how to do it. Of course, it's not easy to evaluate how climate-friendly a product truly is or isn't. This knowledge gap, the second barrier, also leads to a lot of people thinking that climate-friendly products are of poorer quality. They believe that the more climate-friendly a product is, the lower the quality. Subsequently, they stick to what they know because quality and price are still important decision-making factors that many people aren't willing to budge on. We also noticed this in our research in Belgium. Price and quality remain the most important criteria when choosing a brand or product. Sustainability has become the third most important criterium (replacing innovation).

FIGURE 18

Sustainability is the third factor when choosing a brand

(Q: why do you choose a brand, %)

Lack of knowledge about the quality of climate-friendly products complicates matters for young companies in particular. This was proven by scientific research into launches of innovative, climate-friendly products compared with innovative, regular products to see which had a higher rate of success. The hypothesis was that the climate would be the driving factor because it has become such an important issue, but the results were two-sided. Climate-friendly products from unknown brands tend to have less successful launches, because consumers question the quality of unknown products and assume that climate-friendly products are of lower quality. Conversely, new products by brands that have already proven themselves to be climate-friendly tend to enjoy much more successful launches because there is no question as to the quality of the product.[81] This shows once again how important it is to build credibility in the eyes of the consumer in order to be part of the solution.

How can climate-friendly companies overcome this knowledge barrier?

Make it crystal clear

Allbirds, which started as a Kickstarter project, makes wool footwear in the most climate-friendly way possible. Each pair of shoes that you buy from the company comes with an emissions card, which displays the total emissions generated by the product. That's not to say that everyone understands what 7.1kg of CO_2 emissions represents (for comparison, the footprint of a plastic bag is around 1.6kg, while a pair of jeans is responsible for around 29.6 kg of CO_2), but they want to help consumers understand carbon emissions like they currently understand calories. Nobody knows exactly what 2,500 calories represents, but everyone knows that if you exceed that on a daily basis, you will gain weight. For Allbirds' co-CEO, Joey Zwillinger, "carbon dioxide reduction is the most important metric for our business."[82] It is the only way to be sure, as a company, that you are helping the climate and consumers have the right to know what they are buying. The emissions card also has another purpose. By 2025, they want to halve their global footprint in order to reach 'near zero' by 2030. Today they are already climate-neutral, but that is because they offset part of their emissions. They still have work to do to be truly 'near zero' and they want consumers to be able to follow their lead.

FIGURE 19

An Allbirds trainer carbon-footprint card

WOOL PIPER	
MATERIALS	+5.7 kg CO₂e
MANUFACTURING	+1.1 kg CO₂e
USE	+0.1 kg CO₂e
END OF LIFE	+0.2 kg CO₂e
TOTAL	**+7.1 kg CO₂e**

Allbirds transportation emissions are calculated separately and our entire footprint is offset to zero.

In order to calculate the quantity of emissions they produce per shoe, they created an emissions calculator. This takes into account the materials used, as well as manufacture, transport, use by the consumer and lifespan. Undertaking all the analyses needed to create this kind of calculator is a serious investment. Nevertheless, on Earth Day 2021, they made their calculation tool available to everyone, even their competitors. Their reason for doing so was simple: they want to see more emissions cards on the market. This would allow consumers to have a point of comparison and better evaluate the emissions generated by different pairs of shoes. "We would be thrilled to hear that other brands come out with products with lower emissions than ours," says their co-CEO. Allbirds makes climate-friendly footwear. For them, it is important for consumers to be able to see how climate-friendly their shoes really are. The more consumers understand that value, the better their footwear will sell. This means that climate emissions cards are a strategic tool for them to share knowledge and lower that barrier.

In 2021, Mastercard surveyed 85% of its clients to explore how they could tackle the climate crisis. 42% of respondents said they wanted to better understand how they could make more climate-friendly purchases. At the same time, Mastercard set itself a very ambitious climate target: net-zero by 2040. Net-zero means cutting greenhouse gas emissions to as close to zero as possible and balancing any remaining emissions by removing them from the atmosphere, thanks to oceans and forests for instance. According to the GHG Protocol Corporate Standard, a company's greenhouse gas emissions are classified in three scopes. It is mandatory to report scope 1 and 2 emissions, but scope 3 is voluntary and also the hardest to monitor.

! Scope 1 includes direct CO_2 emissions, produced by corporate buildings, transport and production-related activities. This includes the CO_2 emitted by factory machines or office heating, for example.

! Scope 2 encompasses all the emissions generated by the production of the energy that is purchased. These emissions don't occur on the company's premises or manufacturing lines, but are produced by the energy supplier. That's why they're called indirect emissions.

! Scope 3 includes everything that doesn't fall under either scope 1 or 2. It covers emissions produced by using raw or other materials and, most importantly, the emissions produced by the use of a company's products after sale. These emissions are generated in the supply chain and by customers. That is why they are so hard to monitor.

Mastercard wants to lower these 'scope 3' emissions by 25% by 2025. It's thus in their best interest if their customers shop in a climate-friendly way, which means that the faster the knowledge barrier is tackled, the better. Mastercard's answer is a carbon calculation tool, which shows customers how much CO_2 was emitted for each purchase and lets them see whether their monthly footprint has increased or decreased at the end of every month. If customers think things aren't moving fast enough, they can make a one-off donation to Mastercard's tree-planting project to help pick up the pace. It's an initiative that clearly shows how a company's self-interest can neatly coincide with consumer interest and how dismantling the knowledge barrier can play in everybody's favour.

FIGURE 20

Oda climate emissions list from past shopping trips

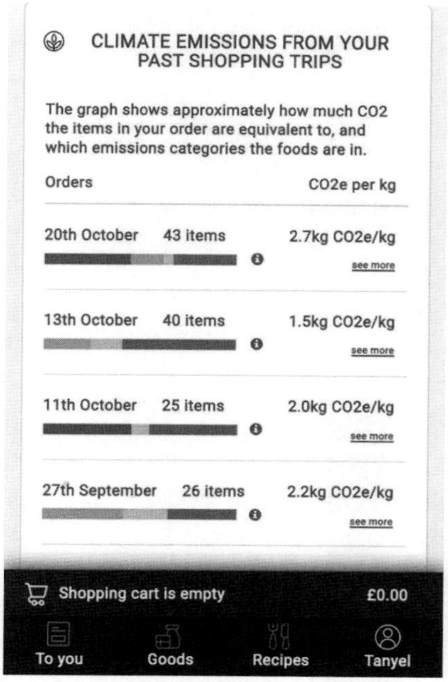

Another company responding to its customers' desire for better understanding of what is and what isn't climate-friendly is an online supermarket in Norway, called Oda. Their initiative has had such a great impact that it's succeeded in curtailing orders for red meat, a direct effect of enhancing customer knowledge. They do this by giving customers a climate receipt which mentions not just the price of the food items purchased but also the CO_2 emissions. In order to better show customers how much or how little, say, 2.7 kg of CO_2 per kilogram is (see figure 20), they group all products into four different emissions categories: low, medium, high and very high. These are illustrated with colours (green, yellow, orange and red). They use data from Cicero (Centre for International Climate Research), a Norwegian centre for climate research that calculates emissions over the whole life cycle of a product. Customers can thus see the impact of their product choices on the planet and, given that Oda gives this information for all purchases, they can also monitor how their own behaviour is changing.

It allows consumers to make different choices, which the company has verified with their own eyes. Since they launched the climate receipt, meat sales have dropped while sales of meat alternatives have grown by 80% and customers buy 50% more fruit and vegetables. It shows once again that customers will adopt more climate-friendly behaviour if they are given enough information to base their choices on.

FIGURE 21

People are increasingly looking for information related to biodiversity

Google searches for terms related to biodiversity and nature loss, relative to all searches, index value yearly average

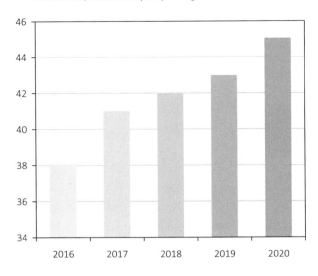

Finally, Oda's own climate agenda also plays a role for the climate. They want to halve CO_2 emissions by 2025, which means that every kg of CO_2 that is not emitted thanks to the climate receipt is also good news for them. In the meantime, Oda's climate receipts have become so popular that other Norwegian supermarkets are also jumping on the bandwagon. It should come as no surprise that climate labels are finding so much success among consumers. Research by the Economist Intelligence Unit (EIU) shows that consumers actively seek information about the climate impact of the products they buy: since 2016, the number of Google searches for sustainable goods has risen by 71% worldwide, with no let-up in growth during the COVID-19 pandemic.[83]

This hasn't escaped the notice of **Amazon.com** either, which has introduced a sustainable section on its website. This allows customers to browse roughly 40,000 products bearing the logo 'Climate Pledge Friendly'. That logo can only be earned if a number of international institutions certify that a company is climate-friendly, but Amazon decides which companies can be featured there and which can't. People who don't trust Amazon's selection process can use **Finch**, which has coded a Chrome browser extension powered by machine learning to sort Amazon products based on their climate impact. This sorting is done using objective, scientific data. Microsoft Bing has also experienced a sharp rise in sustainable searches, and thus show **Good On You** results with its search results. This Australian-based app rates fashion brands based on three criteria: environment, people and animals. More than 3,000 brands are currently included, each with a rating of 'very good', 'good', 'it's a start', 'not good enough' and 'avoid'. If you're using the app, you can scan a product barcode to see the rating. On Bing, you can see this rating in your search results when searching for a product. The app welcomes you with the slogan "Wear the change you want to see" every time you scan a product. If that product doesn't score well, the app will suggest a more sustainable alternative.

Mobile apps that aim to help consumers understand exactly what they are buying are starting to spring up like mushrooms. If a company says that it is climate-friendly, you can find out whether that statement is true or not by simply scanning the barcode. In France, the **Clear Fashion** app measures the positive and negative impact of fashion brands on the climate, people, health and animals. You can view the results with a quick scan of the product's barcode and the app also allows you to compare products. They've already rated more than 10,000 branded products.

The **Yuka** app, which is also French, has been downloaded by 24 million users in 12 countries. By scanning the label, users can see a score based on the product's nutritional value, climate impact and carbon emissions. This app is also changing the purchasing behaviour of consumers and, as a result, the strategy of producers. French supermarket chain, Intermarché, has already adapted the recipes of 900 of its own-brand food products in order to score better on Yuka. The **Giki** mobile app helps climate-aware customers in the United Kingdom find sustainable and ethical products while they're out and about. The app has more than 250,000 products in its database and 13 'Giki badges', which inform users about the factors that make a product sustainable.

The **GoodGuide** app also has more than 210,000 items in its database and rates each on a scale from 1-10 on the basis of social responsibility, health impact and climate. **Ecountabl**, meanwhile, is an app that allows users to ensure that brands and products align with their personal values. For example, a consumer can select 'gender' or 'climate action' as one of their core values. Once the app is connected with a credit card to evaluate purchases, users can view scores for more than 10,000 brands based on the values they personally find important.

We could continue listing these kinds of apps for a while, as there are so many aiming to provide climate transparency. That's because consumers are not just looking for information, they're also using it as a selection criterium in the purchasing process, both online and offline. Given that there are so many sources of information, more and more companies are choosing to display their own climate label on their products. In 2020, research by Carbon Trust showed that 67% of consumers think it's a good idea for companies to make the climate impact of their products clearly visible on the packaging.[84]

Multinationals are also jumping on the bandwagon. Upfield and Quorn print their climate impact on their product packaging. Unilever said that it wanted to test CO_2 labelling on a select group of products in the US and Europe in 2021. If that goes well, they'll think about rolling out carbon labelling to all 75,000 products.[85] That would create a market-defining surge. Unilever is also considering the idea of 'carbon-neutral' or 'carbon-friendly' supermarket aisles. Retailers could add these sections to their shops, just as they did for 'vegan' and 'vegetarian' areas before. Asda, a supermarket chain in the UK, already has a complete aisle dedicated to vegan products. Nestle, Unilever,

PepsiCo, Danone and a host of other large companies also support the Eco Impact score by Foundation Earth, an alternative to the Ecoscore.

It must be stated that there is scientific support for carbon labelling, but there is a lot of work that remains to be done. According to recent research by Michael P. Vandenberg, Chair of Law at Vanderbilt University, we need more standardisation of the information on climate labels if we are to make them easy to understand for consumers. Some labels display a number, while others use a simple traffic-light symbol to show how one product compares with another. There are other labels that give a number for equivalent greenhouse gas emissions, or CO_2 emissions, showing the quantity of greenhouse gases emitted during the production, transport and use of a product. Some labels show several of these metrics. There is thus a need for this information to be standardised and simplified. Hopefully, the EU will be able to help with this by the end of 2022. Nevertheless, the most important conclusion we can draw concerning emissions labels is that, in addition to enhancing consumer knowledge and strengthening the reputation of a brand, they also help companies cut emissions. Finally, labels often also help reduce costs. Companies that calculate their climate impact tend to identify efficiency improvements that are easy to implement. Four birds with one stone.

Although most examples can be found in the food and fashion industries, which through no coincidence are two industries with very high emissions, emissions labels are popping up everywhere. Cross-product initiatives such as Ecoscore and Eco Impact exist, but brands also see this as a point of contact with the consumer that they can use to stand out from the competition. Labels strengthen the position of a company as part of the solution and are a tool that can be used to reduce the credibility deficit. Climate labels are thus much more than a number. They are spearheading the climate race, as they allow consumers to identify which side a company is on. Sharing your net-zero plan with consumers can also help them understand that you are on the right side.

Take them with you to zero

"F*ck you CO_2."[86] That's how BrewDog let the world know, in spectacular fashion, that it is carbon-negative. BrewDog is the most well-known, but also most controversial, British brewery. They call themselves a "post-punk, apocalyptic motherfucker of a craft brewery".[87] It was founded in 2007 in Aberdeenshire by two friends, James Watt and Martin Dickie. Since then, BrewDog has grown into a multinational company with nearly 100 locations and more than 1,000 employees throughout the world. BrewDog is built on a corporate counter-culture: it positions itself as a brewery by and for 'punks', an army of 180,000 crowdfunding investors who invested more than 80 million pounds and thus gave the brothers the opportunity to build their own brewery. They have caused quite a bit of controversy. In the run-up to the Winter Olympic Games, they launched a beer called 'Hello my name is Vladimir' to openly protest Russia's ban on 'homosexual propaganda'. They also launched the 'BrewDog Viagra' beer in response to Kate Middleton and Prince William's wedding.

FIGURE 22

BrewDog announcing it is carbon negative

On 24th August 2020, however, BrewDog announced that it was carbon-negative. Being carbon-negative means that it is removing more carbon from the atmosphere than it is putting into it. This plan came about after a meeting with Sir David Attenborough, who made the founding duo realise just how urgent the problem is and how they can do something to solve it. That's exactly what they did, becoming the first international brewery to achieve carbon-negative status. How did they do it? First, they invested in several emissions-cutting measures, such as using biomethane – namely malted barley, a natural by-product of brewing beer – as an alternative to fossil fuels.

They also make sure that the electricity they use to brew beer in the UK comes straight from local wind turbines. A bio-installation uses anaerobic fermentation to turn the brewery's waste water into clean H_2O and biomethane. They offset any emissions they haven't been able to avoid by planting trees. In this way, they remove twice as much carbon as they emit and can call themselves carbon-negative.[88] They introduced their tree-planting plan with the same boundless energy. They decided to plant 'the largest forest ever' in Scotland.

FIGURE 23

BrewDog announces it's planting the biggest forest ever

To do this, the company bought 50 km² of land near Loch Lomond where they will plant more than a million trees. The forest still needs to be planted, so a lot of CO_2 is not yet being compensated for. That's why they also work with projects in the rest of the world. They're even getting their customers involved. In early 2021, they launched the 'Buy one, get one tree' project. As a BrewDog customer, you can scan the QR code on the bottle or can you just bought to let BrewDog know they have to plant a tree. The marketers at BrewDog understand marketing. They saw the launch of their plan to cut emissions as an opportunity to give the brand the credibility it needed to be perceived as part of the solution. That's in stark contrast to most net-zero plans, which are launched as a simple press release.

NET-ZERO PLANS DESERVE MORE THAN A SIMPLE PRESS RELEASE.

"The planet is facing a serious climate and nature crisis and this requires extraordinary action. According to our values as a company, we strive to do more than most, so that's why we have developed Lifetime Carbon Neutral. It's an innovative commitment involving a 20-year partnership with WWF International to capture the equivalent of our historical carbon emissions by 2041. We will also dramatically reduce our future CO_2 emissions and ask our suppliers to do the same. Hopefully other companies will be inspired to become 'Lifetime Carbon Neutral' in order to create a sustainable future for all," stated David Briggs, CEO of the VELUX Group.[89] It sounds like a press release, because that's exactly what it is. It also sounds complicated: lifetime carbon neutral. What's wrong with net-zero?

FIGURE 24

Velux announcing its Lifetime Carbon Neutral plan

Unlike BrewDog, Velux is a company that does not want to make a spectacle. This global leader in skylights, founded in Copenhagen, never makes the news. In September 2020, however, they did just that and they did it on purpose. That press release was the start of a full-blown campaign, in which all the pieces of the puzzle came together. They said that by 2041, their one-hundredth birthday, they would remove all of the carbon that they had emitted to date from the air and that any carbon they emitted between now and 2030 would be reduced to zero. By 2041, they will be Lifetime Carbon

Neutral. They even explained how they're going to do it. Their total historic footprint – 5.6 million tonnes of CO_2 emitted since it was founded in 1941 – will be compensated for through forest conservation projects led by the WWF. Any further CO_2 emitted by the company and its value chain (covering scopes 1, 2 and 3) will, according to science-based targets, be brought in line with the 1.5°C reduction target in the Paris Agreement and reduced to zero.

Velux is thus taking responsibility not just for the future, but also for the past. That's a unique and massive commitment which has allowed the company to become one of the most prominent climate leaders in the business sector. It's also a huge challenge. Try going back in time to try to find out how much CO_2 you've emitted since, let's say, 1957. Of course, Velux is not doing this alone. It's working with the WWF to reforest and conserve forests and with the Carbon Trust to make sure that everything is scientifically and numerically correct. WWF and Carbon Trust are the crucial third parties that give this project the credibility it needs. Thanks to this initiative, Velux is making a great leap toward obtaining the title of a climate-friendly company. Everyone who has seen the campaign and wants to build sustainably knows where they'd best order their skylights. Meanwhile, Velux's marketers made the most of the net-zero plan to firmly position the company as part of the solution, in a credible way, and draw the general public with them.

"Hello Edan." On the screen, you see a baby alone in a large double bed, looking so small. "What a beautiful name". The bed is in a loft. Through the window, you can see and hear cars driving past. We must be in a city. "It means magic." You can't really make out whether the baby is a boy or a girl. You can't guess from the name either, Edan is a gender-neutral name. My gut feeling is that it's a girl, who's just been welcomed into the world. Edan's sleeping. When the voice calls her name, she fidgets a little as if in response. "You don't know us. You won't understand what we're about to say. But one day, Edan, you will. Because we want to make you a promise. We want to be held to it. And every year, for years to come, we'll remain committed to it." A piano starts playing softly, a peaceful melody, the kind of melody that makes tears well in your eyes. "A promise between you and us and the planet. We promise that everything we make, the way we make it, and even how you use it will be carbon-neutral by your tenth birthday." The camera focuses on the baby's face. The voice says: "Promise." The baby's eyes open, as if they heard and understood that promise. At the end of the ad, the Apple logo appears with the website www.apple.com/2030. It's the kind of video that stops you in your tracks.

FIGURE 25

Apple announcing carbon neutrality by 2030

That's how Apple decided to announce its climate plans. Less spectacular than some, but it hits Apple users right at the heart. Apple is making considerable efforts to reduce their carbon emissions but, as is the case for so many technological companies, it's not feasible to reduce them to absolutely nothing. They're also looking to the benefits that nature's solutions can offer us. Together with Conservation International (CI) and Goldman Sachs, they founded the Restore Fund, with a budget of 200 million dollars to invest in natural climate solutions. With that money, they want to remove at least 1 million tonnes of carbon from the atmosphere per year to ensure that they are climate-neutral by 2030.

Apple, Velux and BrewDog are three companies that have each shared their net-zero plans with consumers in their own way, successfully positioning themselves as climate-friendly companies that are part of the solution. Is that perception something they have definitively obtained for the long-term? Obviously that's not how it works, but it's a first step toward building up their credibility.

You may have noticed that while Apple promises carbon neutrality, Velux promises lifetime carbon neutrality and BrewDog promises carbon negativity. How can consumers make sense of these terms? We're being bombarded with a whole bunch of jargon and concepts, such as net-zero, climate neutrality, climate-positive and carbon-negative. The answer, however, is simple: consumers can't make sense of it. It's like the wild wild west, everyone has their own take. On the one hand, that's good because it means that a company can differentiate itself, but it's not ideal either because it can lead to too much confusion. In order to prevent any confusion, scientists have clearly defined all these terms, (see table 4). It would be nice if companies could abide by these definitions in order for climate-friendly behaviour to gain ground as quickly as possible among consumers. The faster it becomes clear to the consumer what is meant by net-zero, climate-neutral or even climate-positive, the more companies will be in a position to build up the credibility they need to be part of the solution.

TABLE 4

List of climate-friendly claims

Climate claims	
Net-zero emissions	The achievement of a state in which an entity removes as many greenhouse gas emissions from the atmosphere as it causes (IPCC, 2018)
Climate neutrality	State in which an entity's actions has no net effect on the surrounding climate; used especially with reference to the global climate system (IPCC, 2018). While carbon neutrality applies to carbon dioxide emissions, climate neutrality applies to all anthropogenic greenhouse-gas emissions (Levin, Song and Morgan, 2015).
Net-zero CO_2 emissions	The achievement of a state in which any remaining carbon dioxide emissions produced by an entity are cancelled by offsetting (IPCC, 2018)
Carbon neutrality	State in which an entity's actions result in net-zero carbon dioxide emissions (IPCC, 2018)
Zero-carbon	Similar to "carbon-free", zero-emissions implies that an entity emits no carbon dioxide emissions.
Carbon-free	Technically implies the absence of carbon dioxide emissions, but often used as a synonym for carbon neutrality (Colenbrander *et al.,* 2019)
Net-negative emissions	A state in which an entity removes more emissions from the atmosphere than it produces; can refer to carbon dioxide emissions specifically or greenhouse-gas emissions more broadly (IPCC, 2018)
Carbon-negative	Synonym for net-negative emissions, but typically refers only to carbon dioxide emissions
Climate-positive	Similar to net-negative emissions, climate-positive suggests that an entity removes more greenhouse-gas emissions than it produces.
Emissions-free	Producing no emissions; can refer either to carbon dioxide emissions specifically, or greenhouse-gas emissions more broadly
Zero-emissions	Synonym for emissions-free

Like an emissions label, a net-zero plan is also a spearhead in the fight for cli-mate-friendly consumption, while helping to close the gap in the credibility deficit. How many companies already have net-zero plans? 2021 was a record year for the SBTi (the Science Based Target Initiative), a global organisation that helps companies, like Velux, to develop their net-zero plans in line with the latest scientific insights. It's a collaboration between CDP, a non-profit organisation, the United Nations Global Compact, the World Resources Insti-tute (WRI) and the WWF. The aim of SBTi is to help companies meet the targets of the Paris Agreement. In 2021, the number of companies taking part doubled to 2,253, spread across 70 countries and 15 sectors and repre-senting more than a third of the world's market capitalisation.[90] That's a third of the total market value of the shares outstanding of all listed companies in the world. It seems we're getting somewhere.

But not fast enough. In the EU, only 16% of companies have a net-zero plan in line with the 1.5 degree target.[91] Do we know what companies that don't have net-zero plans emit? Not really. Worldwide, 63% of businesses share no or only partial emissions data.[92] This means that nobody knows where these companies stand or whether they're helping or hindering the achievement of the Paris Agreement. In January 2022, thanks to research by PwC, we finally found out how many companies have a net-zero plan worldwide: only 22%. We also don't know whether those plans were developed in accordance with SBTi principles. What's worrying is that nearly six in ten (57%) CEOs with no net-zero plan think that they don't need one because their greenhouse gas emissions are negligible (see figure 26). How can they know? The study also revealed that 55% claim not to have the capabilities to measure their emissions.[93] Reading that as a climate scientist, it gives you a bad taste in your mouth. That's not good news at all. Not for companies themselves, nor for the business sector as a whole. These companies are part of the problem and don't understand why that, in itself, is a problem. As such, they threaten our chances of achieving the Paris Agreement and thus pose a risk to the companies doing their utmost to be part of the solution. It's crucial that more net-zero plans are developed, that sector federations back these plans, ensure that they are designed in accordance with the SBTi rules and implemented properly. That final point is not easy. We're talking about 30-year long pro-jects. Not many business projects have such a long timeframe, which is why publishing net-zero plans is a good thing. It's not just to generate credibility among consumers in order to be seen as part of the solution but also, once published, to make it harder to deviate from the plan. It's only realistic to expect that between now and 2050 something or other may go wrong and that the desire to scale back those plans may become just a bit too tempting.

FIGURE 26

Firms without decarbonisation commitments cite lack of emissions and capabilities

Question: How accurate are the following statements regarding why your company has not made a carbon-neutral or net-zero commitment?

(Showing only 'very accurate' and 'extremely accurate' responses)

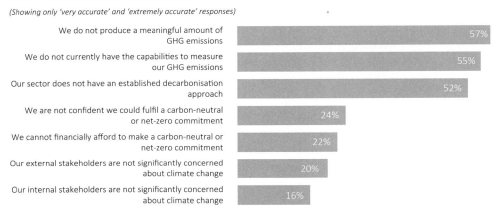

We do not produce a meaningful amount of GHG emissions	57%
We do not currently have the capabilities to measure our GHG emissions	55%
Our sector does not have an established decarbonisation approach	52%
We are not confident we could fulfil a carbon-neutral or net-zero commitment	24%
We cannot financially afford to make a carbon-neutral or net-zero commitment	22%
Our external stakeholders are not significantly concerned about climate change	20%
Our internal stakeholders are not significantly concerned about climate change	16%

Another danger is that the people writing the plans today won't be the ones completing the implementation thereof in 2050, especially not the CEO. That's a significant risk: leadership changes bring changes. A CEO who makes a net-zero promise today for the company they represent will not be the CEO who actually implements the plan, nor will the next CEO or the one after that. That's a huge risk. Nevertheless, as mentioned before, the first priority must be to have more net-zero plans. Today, these are being made on a voluntary basis. At COP26, then Chancellor of the Exchequer of the United Kingdom, Rishi Sunak, announced that every company listed on the British stock market would be legally obliged to create annual climate plans, or risk financial sanctions. In the EU, there will also be similar obligations and sanctions from 2024. The business sector must understand that net-zero plans in business have become a political tool that governments use to achieve their own net-zero plans. No country will ever renege on its commitment to become net-zero. There is no way back. In order to understand the dynamics behind that, we need to go back to 2013, two years before the Paris Agreement was signed. That's when the idea of net-zero began to gain ground, ensuring its current status as an international political norm.

FIGURE 27

Cumulative climate goal mentions in newspapers from 2010 until 2021

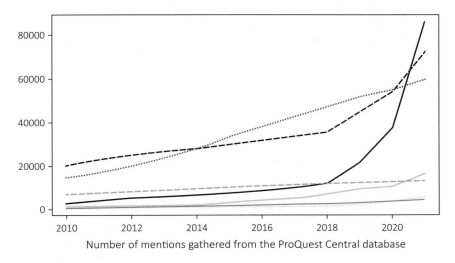

Number of mentions gathered from the ProQuest Central database

Goal searched
— Net-zero   ⋯⋯ 2 degrees   --- ppm
--- Carbon Neutrality   — 1.5 degrees   ⋯⋯ Climate Neutrality   — Carbon budget

Farhana Yamin, the climate activist we talked about in chapter one, was the first person to call for a net-zero standard.[94] She found that debate in the international community about fixing the climate target at 1.5 or 2 degrees was much too vague. Nobody really understood what 1.5 degrees more or less meant. As a result, it was difficult to impress the importance of these targets on policy makers and it was truly time for policy makers to take urgent action once again. The trauma of 'Flopenhagen' had not yet been forgotten. She also found the whole concept of net-zero much better than the idea of 1.5°C or 2°C, because it clearly states what needs to happen. Everyone must become net-zero. That statement is crystal clear. Saying that everyone must aim for 1.5 degrees, however, is not clear at all. Her idea was seconded by Laurence Tubiana who headed the Institute of Sustainable Development and International Relations (IDDRI) in Paris at the time. Two years later, Tubiana became the French Climate Change Ambassador and Special Representative for COP21. In that capacity, her contributions were absolutely vital to concluding the Paris Agreement. In 2013, she asked Yamin to write a paper about the net-zero concept that was then picked up by NGOs, think-tanks and academics. At that time, a lot of different climate jargon was being used (see table 4), terms such as 'carbon budget', 'climate neutrality', 'ppm' (parts per million) and '1.5 degrees'. In 2018, 'carbon neutrality' and '2 degrees' were attracting the most attention. However, from then on, 'net-zero' started to gain in popularity, eventually becoming the international standard it is today. That is also evident in the way in which the international community understands it. Net-zero has become the benchmark to show how willing a country is to take action and it's working. As is clearly shown in figure 28, only 12 countries had considered or committed to net-zero targets in 2018. By the end of 2021, that rose to 150 countries with net-zero promises, representing 89% of global carbon emissions.

FIGURE 28

Distribution of net-zero targets from 2018 to May 2022

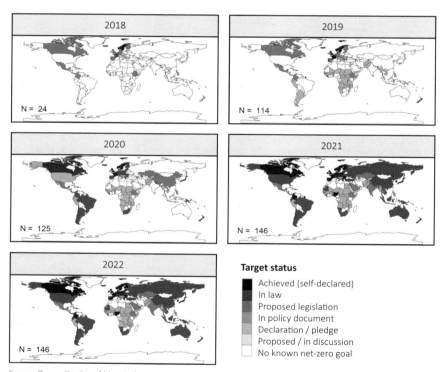

Source: Own collection of historical net-zero targets, based on 2021 data from netzerotracker.com. Map generated in R using the tmaps package

The only way these countries can keep their promises is by reducing their own activities to net-zero, but that's not enough. They need the support of consumers and the business sector in order to succeed. That's why more and more governments will make corporate net-zero plans a legal requirement.

GOVERNMENTS WILL MAKE CORPORATE NET-ZERO PLANS A LEGAL REQUIREMENT

Make any offsetting clear

In January 2020, Shell launched a campaign in the UK promising that you could drive carbon-neutral by filling your tank at a Shell station. All you had to do was fill up using your Shell customer card, Shell Go+. How could they make such a promise? After all, Shell sells fossil fuels and the main cause of the climate crisis is the burning of fossil fuels, by driving a car for example. Shell's answer was carbon-offsetting. They claimed to have worked out how much CO_2 is emitted from 'source to wheel', from the moment fuel is extracted from the ground to someone filling up at the fuel station. They said they would offset all of those emissions by planting trees in Indonesia, Peru and the US. The campaign raised many questions and was even the subject of a number of complaints to the British Advertising Standards Authority (ASA), a government watchdog. After investigating the complaints, the ASA asked Shell to stop their campaign. They concluded that Shell had engaged in misleading advertising with illegal environmental claims.[95] The campaign also ran in the Netherlands but instead of using their customer card, customers could drive carbon-neutral by paying 1 cent more per litre. Nine Dutch students filed a complaint. They had calculated the quantity of emissions Shell could offset if their customers paid 1 cent more per litre, which revealed that the result was 6.2 times too low to be able to compensate for their total emissions. Shell made it look like carbon-offsetting was the magic solution to the climate crisis. In effect, they were saying: If you have enough money in the kitty to plant trees, you're fine. It's greenwashing of the worst kind that absolutely doesn't help the world make a step in the right direction.

Carbon-offsetting is vital in the fight against climate change. It's a tactic any company can use to neutralise its emissions if it can't prevent them. Given that it is virtually impossible for a company to reduce its emissions completely, every net-zero plan can, according to scientists, combine measures to reduce and offset emissions. Companies should ensure that their total emissions are cut by 80 to 90%, while the remaining 10 to 20% can be compensated for. The end result is therefore net-zero: all remaining emissions are offset and thus neutralised.

There are two ways to offset emissions. One makes use of nature. The Earth's surface and the oceans act as enormous carbon sinks, while trees help carbon reach those sinks. The more widespread tree cover on Earth, the larger the sink. Conserving and extending forests are thus two primary methods for offsetting emissions that incidentally also tackle biodiversity loss. Furthermore, technological options should be used to support natural solutions to remove carbon from the air. Nature doesn't have the capacity to offset them all. The Net Zero Tracker, an independent research consortium, keeps track of the quantity and quality of net-zero targets around the whole world. They found that 91% of country targets, 79% of city targets, 78% of regional targets and 48% of targets made by companies listed on the stock market don't specify whether offsetting will be used as part of their net-zero plans. Even among companies that state they will use natural and technological offsetting to a certain extent as part of their net-zero target, 66% don't explain under what conditions.[96] The global balance of compensation versus reduction is thus unclear. Moreover, given the lack of clarity on the topic, it's often seen as a form of greenwashing. That's why organisations like the Science Based Targets initiative and Race to Zero don't allow any offsetting that would replace or delay reductions.

Marketers must tread carefully. Not long ago, a banana brand made a mistake when adding a 'CO_2-neutral' sticker to their logo. They had overlooked the fact that the origin of their bananas, Costa Rica, was also noted on their brand sticker. What happened next was to be expected. The criticism on social media was deafening. A tweet revealed one of the most cynical reactions: "How sweet, they must have cycled here." The brand could have avoided this backlash by explaining that they were offsetting emissions with tree-planting projects, but of course you can't fit that on a sticker. By not sharing that information, consumers were under the impression that the brand was talking about complete reduction, which no-one believed for a second. There is a lack of knowledge about how companies offset their emissions, but that's no reason not to share the details. There are enough consumers who do understand and, as we know from our own research, when consumers find out that brands are greenwashing, half of them will spread the news. By not explaining how you offset your emissions, you're positioning yourself as a greenwasher. Once you've been given that label, it will take a lot of time and effort to shed it. Fortunately, many companies are handling it well.

Carbon-neutral eggs – that's what you can expect by the end of this year from Morrisons, the third largest grocers in the UK. As part of their plan to reduce CO_2 emissions caused by their agricultural supply chain, they want to sell carbon-neutral eggs in their shops. To do that, they will provide their ten largest egg suppliers with small insect-breeding containers. These containers will be fully autonomous, driven by AI, and the insects will be fed with waste from Morrisons' fruit and vegetable processing factories in Yorkshire.[97] Thanks to this initiative, 320,000 free-range chickens on ten farms will be fed insects, supplemented with British beans, peas and sunflower seeds, instead of their usual soy-based feed. Traditionally, insects are a natural food source for chickens, while the soy-based feed that's often used instead is responsible for more than 85% of an egg's carbon footprint. If the pilot project on these ten chicken farms is successful, Morrisons will roll it out across all 60 farms, thus saving a little less than 35,000 tonnes of CO_2 per year, equivalent to the emissions produced by 16,500 cars.

Finding innovative methods to reduce their carbon emissions is indispensable for Morrisons. They want to fully implement their net-zero plan by 2040. To do that, they aim to reduce all carbon emissions from their own activities to zero by 2035 and cut the emissions generated by the supply chain of their own-brand goods by 30% by 2030. The insect project is part of that. These kinds of solutions require a lot of energy upfront but will require them to offset fewer emissions at the end of the day. David Potts, Morrisons' CEO, said: "As a supermarket we depend on a healthy planet to produce the goods we sell to customers. We've committed to removing carbon emissions, rather than setting a carbon-neutral target that would depend heavily on offsetting."[98] The man is right. We need to reduce our emissions. Offsetting is merely a tool that can assist us and must be used as such. An article in the New York Times wrote: "When companies rely on them to offset their emissions, they risk merely hitting the climate "snooze" button, kicking the can to future generations who will have to deal with those emissions."[99]

EASE

The third barrier preventing climate-friendly behaviour from becoming more widespread, is that such behaviour is still just a bit too difficult for the majority of people. Companies that are a part of the solution have come up with ways to make climate-friendly behaviour a bit easier for consumers.

Don't make a big deal of replacements

The best way to make things easy for the consumer is to replace a not climate-friendly product with a climate-friendly alternative. Cleansing wipes sold by **Boots** in the UK are a good example.[100] With sales of more than 800 million units across 140 product lines of skincare, baby, tissue and healthcare, this drugstore chain is one of the largest sellers of wet wipes in the United Kingdom. They represent around 15% of all wipe sales in the UK. On Earth Day 2022, the company announced that it would stop selling wet cleansing wipes containing plastic fibres by the end of 2022. They will be replaced with biodegradable wipes made of plant materials. Rather than sell a climate-friendly version alongside a less climate-friendly option while trying to convince customers to choose the plant-based version, they've instead chosen to remove the not climate-friendly option from the equation altogether. Simple. This makes things easy for the consumer and equates to 800 million not climate-friendly products being removed from the consumption chain in one fell swoop. It's a great example of the scale of change we need.

Make sure items have a second life

For years, buying vintage and second-hand goods was preferred by people who couldn't, or weren't willing to, pay for a new item. Today it's a climate-friendly statement. That hasn't escaped the notice of a large range of companies, who are now bringing their own solutions to the table to allow more people to buy second-hand goods more easily. Second-hand sales of luxury goods are a perfect example, as they are growing five times faster than sales of new luxury goods, according to a report by Bain & Company in late 2021.[101] Consumers looking for luxury seem to embrace 'pre-loved' options. Between 2017 and 2021, sales of second-hand luxury goods rose by 67% representing a total of 33 billion euros. During the same period, sales of new luxury goods rose by only 12%. Even though the market as a whole dropped by 29% in 2020, during the coronavirus pandemic, the second-hand market continued to grow. This means that 11.7% of all luxury-good sales in 2021 were second-hand. Luxury clothing brands used to prefer seeing their pieces ending up in landfill rather than a second-hand shop, but that's no longer the case. In December 2020, **Gucci** opened its own second-hand shop on the online retailer TheRealReal.[102] **Oscar de la Renta, Valentino** and other premium brands have followed suit.

FIGURE 29

Change in global sales of luxury goods since 2017

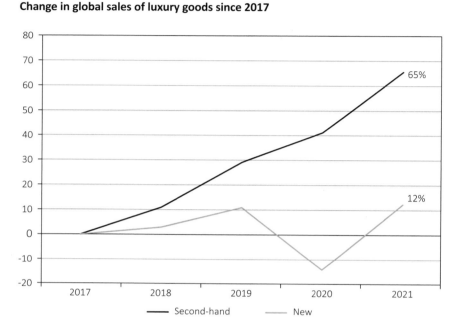

When consumers buy second-hand, they ensure that fewer valuable raw materials are extracted from the Earth, while reducing the mountain of textile waste and lowering the quantity of fossil fuels leeching into the atmosphere. This climate argument is important to brands and they can also benefit from the resulting income of managing their own second-hand sales. They all have climate plans that they need to achieve and second-hand goods clearly play a role in that plan by lengthening the lifespan of an item. But the fact that consumers expect this type of action is even more important to their plan; 68% of consumers believe that the fashion industry has a responsibility toward the climate and must take that seriously.

Six in ten consumers also think that fashion brands need to help them dress in a more climate-friendly way.[103] If a fashion brand wants to make sure that they are part of the solution, they need to help consumers do this. Of course, brands can also produce new products that are more climate-friendly, while responding to demand for second-hand items. The scale of change that is needed is clear; sales of second-hand goods currently represent 11% of the market and that figure is rising. That's good news for brands and the climate.

"Furniture deserves many lives. Sell us your old **IKEA** furniture on Black Friday and we'll give it another life. #buybackfriday". That's how an Ikea Black Friday video ad ended in 2021. Not the usual 'here are the unbelievable discounts that are only available on Black Friday so get your credit card out now'. Black Friday generates completely artificial and incredibly unnecessary excesses of consumption and is probably the worst sales time of the year for the climate. A British financial website estimated that Black Friday produced more than 429,000 tonnes of carbon emissions in 2020 alone, the equivalent of more than 435 return flights from London to New York or 0.12% of the UK's annual greenhouse gas emissions.[104]

That's just climate nonsense. More and more companies are distancing themselves from the hype of Black Friday, just like Ikea when it decided to run an alternative, more climate-friendly offer: sell your old furniture back to us and we'll give it a second life. Interested consumers could check how much Ikea would give them for their old furniture on the website and received a voucher when they brought the furniture back to the shop. The campaign ran from 24th November to 3rd December 2021. In total, 482,000 price estimates were requested during that period, resulting in 2.1 billion euros of vouchers being handed out.[105] The campaign was so successful, it was extended in many countries.

FIGURE 30

IKEA ad for Black Friday 2021

This buyback initiative was no accident. It fits into Ikea's climate plan, of which one of the targets is to be circular and climate-positive by 2030. The company's "Buyback & Resell" programme helps them extend the lifespan of their products, thus cutting back on production and ensuring that fewer items end up in landfill. Giving their products several lives can also serves to disassociate growth from a negative climate impact, which is the case for Ikea. As a company, it is responsible for 0.1% of global greenhouse gas emissions, of which 42% come from the extraction and processing of raw materials.[106] Reselling existing products can thus help reduce that volume.

Make any non-climate-friendly behaviour unnecessary

Making existing climate-friendly behaviour easier for customers, as we've just seen, is one option for companies, but another is to prevent any behaviour that isn't climate-friendly. You can make it unnecessary.

Rinsing dirty dishes before you put them in the dishwasher is a prime example of non-climate-friendly behaviour. For many people, this is the most normal task in the world and I'm sure many of us have witnessed, or even engaged in, this kind of behaviour at home. We do it to make sure that our dishes come out of the dishwasher sparkling clean. Marketers at **Finish**, Reckit Benckiser's dishwasher detergent, researched the issue and were able to pinpoint exactly how bad it is for the environment. Roughly 75 litres of water is used pre-rinsing dishes for one dishwasher load. That is huge. In the US alone, three in four dishwasher users rinse their dishes before putting them in the dishwasher; convincing them not to do that anymore could save more than 150 billion litres of water per year. Given that we will experience water shortages in the years to come, pre-rinsing must be avoided. That's why Finish's innovation labs developed a new enzyme technology that makes rinsing unnecessary. To market the product, they set up a widespread 'Skip the Rinse' campaign, partnering with National Geographic and The Nature Conservancy, to bring attention to this opportunity to save water. Unfortunately we don't know how many people have stopped pre-rinsing their dishes or how much water has been saved thanks to their campaign.

Washing clothing and other fabrics at more than 30 degrees is another example of how product innovation can make a learned behaviour obsolete and thus contribute to significantly decreasing CO_2 emissions. Like in many European countries, the majority of Belgians (more than 60%) still tend to do laundry at more than 30 degrees. One in ten are even convinced that your laundry will only be clean if you wash it at 60 degrees. "Washing at 30 degrees rather than 40 reduces the impact on CO_2 emissions by 35%," said Virginie Helias, manager of sustainable development at Procter & Gamble. "If, throughout Europe, we resolutely decided to do laundry at 30 degrees rather than 40 degrees, we'd save more than 3.6 million tonnes of CO_2 per year. That's like removing two million cars from the roads."[107] That's why **Ariel**, a P&G laundry detergent, launched the European campaign 'Every degree makes a difference' with National Geographic, calling on Ariel users to wash at a colder temperature. In the UK, they launched a campaign with the WWF to encourage users to wash their laundry at 20 degrees.[108]

Make it reusable

Plastic is everywhere today. It's a useful product that is lightweight, cheap and long-lasting. However, it also comes with a heavy climate and environmental cost. Plastic, mostly composed of oil, is responsible for 6% of global oil use. Slightly less than half of all plastic produced is used for consumer packaging. According to UNEP, the UN Environment Programme, the hidden cost of plastic packaging for consumer products is 75 billion dollars per year. That hidden cost includes the greenhouse gases emitted when extracting raw materials, as well as air pollution, biodiversity loss, soil degradation and, predominantly, plastic pollution in our oceans.[109]

Various studies show that consumers are seeking ways in which to limit their plastic use. In the UK, for example, more than six in ten people actively try to avoid single-use plastic as much as possible. We see similar figures among Belgian consumers. It's thus logical that companies might wish to respond to these demands, perhaps by looking for more climate- and nature-friendly packaging options or by making it easier to reuse existing packaging.

There are two different models for reusable and refillable items. The first is the **refill at home** model, which allows consumers to refill the original packaging with new product, after buying the refill product in store or online. One such example is the food supplement brand **Lyma**, that sells supplements in a subscription format. With your first order, you receive a handmade copper storage container that you can then refill with subsequent orders. Some companies sell their refill product as a concentrate, like **Splosh**, an e-commerce platform that sells its household cleaning products as concentrates. With your first order, you receive a refillable bottle. After that, consumers just have to add water to the concentrate and start cleaning. The company has calculated that by using the refillable bottle 20 times, a consumer can produce 95% less packaging waste.

The second model is **Refill on the go**, which uses distribution points in shops. Consumers bring their original package or own container to the shop to fill up. **BarnBulk** in Canada is a very successful example of a supermarket where you bring and fill your own containers. Founded in 2016, it sells more than 4,000 loose products in 265 locations. The idea is that you bring your own box or container that you can then fill up in the shop. This is called Zero-Waste shopping.

In the UK, there are already more than 200 zero-waste shops.[110] They're mostly small, independent shops, but there's enough of them that they have started attracting the attention of large supermarket chains. Waitrose, Marks & Spencer, Morrisons, Asda and Aldi are all testing refill stations in their shops, where you can refill a wide range of products: pasta, rice, cornflakes, tea bags, coffee, frozen fruit and vegetables, detergent, and shampoo.

FIGURE 31

Ecover refill ad

Other brands are coming up with reusable innovations as well. **Ecover** intro-duced bottles that can be reused more than 50 times by customers. Through-out the United Kingdom, they have refill stations for products like washing-up liquid, hand soap, laundry detergent and all-purpose cleaners. The company calls the initiative "Refillution" and says that they saw more demand than ever for this option last year.

Unilever is also working to offer refillable packaging in the UK, while in Aus-tralia, customers can refill Omo and Surf at the supermarket giant, Coles.[111] In Mexico, Unilever has installed refill stations in Walmart stores. It's also opened a refill station in a Carrefour supermarket in Pakistan where custom-ers can fill up their Sunsilk shampoo.

FIGURE 32

Example of a Unilever refill station

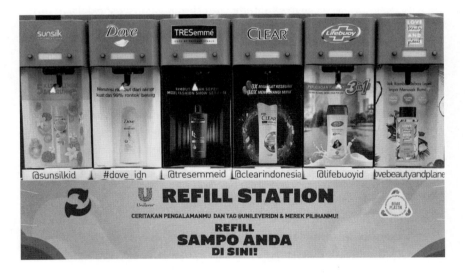

Price, knowledge and ease are the three most-cited barriers that prevent consumers from actively shopping in a climate-friendly way. The afore-mentioned examples demonstrate how various companies are working to overcome those barriers. In so doing, they help strengthen their credibility as a climate-friendly company and as part of the solution. But that alone is obviously not enough; there are also other ways in which companies can be climate-friendly.

NOT ALL CLIMATE-FRIENDLY BRANDS ARE CREATED EQUAL

We have seen that climate-friendly product sales are booming. We've also learned that the overwhelming majority of consumers want to adapt their consumption habits but are hindered by a number of barriers. We've heard from Felix Creutzig who underlined the importance of the business sector dismantling those barriers as quickly as possible, because a change in behaviour could ensure the emissions cuts we need to make a difference and allow us to achieve the Paris Agreement. Although such a shift can't reduce the physical risks of climate change, it can contribute to reducing the transition risks. That's music to the ears of shareholders. Some companies have already understood this reasoning and are doing everything they can to dismantle the barriers for consumers.

This also helps them work toward their own climate plans, especially in terms of scope 3 emissions. Companies like Allbirds and BrewDog exemplify the fact that climate friendliness is becoming an ever more important factor of success. Price and quality are also factors, of course, but for the same price and quality, climate friendliness will be the key to the heart and wallet of consumers. The clearer the negative effects of the climate crisis become, the more doors will open, because consumers want businesses to take the lead in the sustainable transition. They also want companies to ensure that the transition can continue, especially if their finances are put under pressure.

The future is for climate-friendly companies and many are already on the right path. These companies are in transition and that's perfectly normal. Climate friendliness wasn't even on the agenda in board rooms until 2015. Meanwhile, a number of companies are stubbornly sticking to their old ways as part of the problem, partly due to ignorance (what climate problem?), partly due to denial (there is no climate problem!) and partly due to a select few thinking there is no place for them in a climate-friendly world (you can't manage without us!). Nevertheless, some companies are already climate-friendly. These companies have climate friendliness in their DNA and can be categorised in three groups: the 'new climate-friendly companies', the 'refocused climate-friendly companies' and the 'traditional climate-friendly companies' (see figure 33). Let's explore those concepts further.

FIGURE 33

Brand segmentation in times of climate crisis

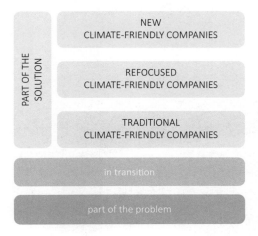

The 'new' climate-friendly companies

"Here are 100 names for your plant-based milk brand. So you can stop using ours." That was the message Kiko Borger, Global Creative Director at NotCo, posted on social media. He also gave some background: "What do you do when one of the biggest players in the food industry uses your name on their plant-based milk brand?" He also made a mobile ad of it (see figure 34). NotCo is the company behind NOTMILK, a plant-based alternative to regular milk. NotCo, founded in 2015, is a Chilean food-technology company that makes plant-based burgers, ice cream and milk. It's the fastest-growing food company in Latin America. Its plant-based 'NotMeat' products are sold in Burger King and Papa John's; the 'Rebel Whopper' is made with their burger.

NotCo uses an AI tool named Giuseppe to make their plant-based products. Giuseppe uses data banks containing thousands of plants and plant-based ingredients, of which there are 300,000 varieties to be found in the plant world. On average, a human being eats 200 different types of plants which means that there's much more to be discovered. By analysing the molecules in food products, it learns which combinations can best replicate the taste, texture and behaviour of existing meat and dairy products. When Giuseppe develops an initial formula, a group of food scientists and chefs make NotCo prototypes that consumers then test based on taste, texture and other criteria, giving their feedback to the system through statements like 'less sugar'. The machine then continues finetuning the recipes based on that feedback. **NOTMILK**, for example, was created by combining precisely the right amounts of pineapple and cabbage so that it heats, foams and freezes just like real milk.[112]

FIGURE 34

NotCo mobile ad

In terms of marketing, they go all out on climate, which is obviously something they can do given that they make plant-based products. In January 2022, however, Alpro – a Danone brand and also a B Corporation – launched a new non-dairy range, called Not M*lk, to supermarket shelves in the United Kingdom. NotCo, also a B Corporation, couldn't stay silent and took to social media to suggest 100s of other names that Alpro could have used for their new product.[113] It's a story that makes me think about Oatly's Mjölk, but we'll come back to that later. NotCo is an example of a company that has found a technological solution to help solve the climate problem: "When we discovered removing animals from food production would protect the planet, we didn't ask why. We asked, why not. Let's create an algorithm that could learn how to combine an infinite combination of plants to replicate the flavour & texture of animal products – without compromising on taste, feel, or function."[114] The fact that they are taking on one of the largest and most high-profile industries is a challenge they're happy to accept.

Dash Water is another new company that has come up with an unexpected, but climate-friendly, solution and immediately taken on the big boys.

FIGURE 35

Dash Water advert

In the soft-drink industry, climate initiatives tend to focus on the recyclability and reusability of packaging. That's why Coca-Cola has invested in a universal, reusable bottle. All established brands were trying to outdo each other in terms of packaging, until **DASH Water**, a B Corporation, broke into the market. Dash produces sparkling water infused with fruit, sold in a can made of fully-recycled aluminium. But the can isn't the focus for Dash. They want to limit food waste. What has water got to do with food waste, you may ask, and it's a question they often get. Their business strategy is to use 'wonky fruit and veg' to make their soft drinks, in other words, fruit and vegetables that don't look good enough to be sold in supermarkets but are just as tasty. Their drinks contain no calories, sugar or sweeteners. In 2020, just three years after their foundation, they sold more flavoured drinks in the UK than San Pellegrino and became the market leader. In 2020, they managed to save

145 tonnes of 'wonky' fruit and vegetables that would otherwise have been wasted. In 2021, this grew to 300 tonnes.

Alex Wright and Jack Scott founded Dash Water in 2017.[115] They both had an agricultural background which confronted them with the reality of food waste in their childhood. Jack's family farm in Shropshire, for example, had a contract with McCain's, the chip manufacturer. They wanted a certain quantity of potatoes to make their chips, which meant that the whole family spent a lot of time sorting potatoes at the end of the summer holidays. However, many potatoes were deemed too small to use. "I always thought it was such a massive waste of time, energy and resources to grow food that we would then throw away," said Jack about the issue. So when Alex and Jack were thinking about what kind of fruit they could use to make their water, they immediately thought of wonky fruit. Dash is now available in more than 5,000 shops throughout Europe and livens up the water aisles in Sainsburys and Waitrose. By 2025, they want to save 2,600 tonnes of wonky fruit and veg from landfill.

"In the last two years, we've kept over five million jugs out of landfill. We're aiming for 700 million. That's our target," said Brad Liski, CEO of **Tru Earth**. They make laundry detergent strips that are 10 centimetres long and 5 centimetres wide. One strip is enough for one load of laundry. The strips are paraben- and phosphate-free, hypoallergenic, biodegradable, contain no animal ingredients and completely dissolve in cold and warm water. While the rest of the industry rattles its brains over the recyclability of bottles and boxes, Tru Earth is removing packaging altogether. The product is a massive hit. Founded in 2019, today they have 690,000 customers in 74 countries. It is the second-fastest-growing company in Canada and that's not gone unnoticed. The current chief operating officer used to work at Keurig and Gillette, the vice president used to work at Dow Chemical, and the marketing and sales directors are from Johnson & Johnson.[116]

NotCo, Dash Water and Tru Earth are companies that are built around a climate-friendly product. They understand that only a drastic change will do given the time we have left, so they've decided to take on large, high-emissions-producing sectors straightaway. Of course, the fact that they're starting as part of the solution, while most of their competitors are in the transition phase, helps. But they're not alone; there are other types of climate-friendly company.

The 'refocused' climate-friendly companies

A milk war is brewing in Sweden. It all started in 2015 with a campaign by Swedish oat milk brand, Oatly, starring Oatly's CEO himself. You saw their CEO playing a keyboard in the middle of an oat field, singing: "It's like milk, but made for humans." He continued with: "Wow, wow, no cow. No, no, no." A catchy tune, for sure, but it was a strange advert that seemed to imply that oat milk is better for human health than cow's milk. With this ad, Oatly launched a direct attack on the whole Swedish milk industry. In response, the industry federation – LRF Mjölk – quickly filed a lawsuit against them. What was Oatly thinking implying that milk isn't made for people? After all, milk is good. Just like everyone else, the Swedish grew up with the adage that a glass of milk a day is good for your health.

Oatly was founded in 1994 by Swedish nutritional scientist, Rickard Öste. A few years earlier, while working at Lund university in Sweden, he discovered oat milk as a milk alternative for people who are lactose intolerant. He worked with oats because they are grown on a large scale in Sweden. Twenty years later, Toni Petersson, the man behind the keyboard, took over as CEO. He saw things differently. He understood that oat milk was a lactose-free alternative to milk, but first and foremost he saw how Oatly could help in the fight against the climate crisis. According to the statistics, oat milk is much better for the climate than cow's milk. He wanted the rest of the world to know that too, so he had the packaging redesigned to bring attention to the climate impact of cow's milk. On their packaging, Oatly stated that humans can get most of the nutrients they need straight from plants. Cow's milk is an unnecessary, highly-polluting alternative contains the same calories and nutrients. To make their point even clearer, Oatly sponsored a music festival in Göteborg in 2015 and dared participants to go without milk for 72 hours. Large banners displayed the slogans "Seriously, who drinks milk at a festival anyway?" and "72 hours without milk, tonnes of CO_2 saved".[117] In the meantime, LRF Mjölk won its lawsuit. Oatly was no longer allowed to refer to its own product as milk or suggest that cow's milk is unhealthy or unfit for human consumption. Oatly published the verdict, making LRF Mjölk look like it was pestering a little challenger. David versus Goliath.

Arla, the biggest name in the milk industry, kicked off a second round in 2018. It started the 'Only milk tastes like milk' campaign. The advert shows office workers drinking coffee with 'Pjölk'. Pjölk looks like fake milk, not real mjölk

CLIMATE-FRIENDLY BRANDS UNDERSTAND ONLY A DRASTIC CHANGE WILL DO, GIVEN THE TIME WE HAVE LEFT

(milk) and the workers don't seem to be enjoying it. It's an obvious reference to Oatly: fake milk that no-one likes. At the end, a voice says: "Milk is milk. Only milk tastes like milk." There were also variations of the campaign with brölk, sölk and trölk, all fake versions of the only true mjölk. Oatly reacted to this campaign by patenting the fake names and putting them on its packaging.

This battle went on for a while, until Oatly decided to places its entire focus on its climate credentials. Its aim was to make itself a part of the solution by depicting the milk industry as part of the problem. It then became a cut-throat competition. Explaining that oat milk is healthier than regular milk didn't work for Oatly anymore. Instead, they wanted to draw attention to the fact that oat milk is plant-based and thus has a much smaller negative impact on the climate than cow's milk. The climate impact of the meat and dairy industry is colossal, as they're responsible for 60% of the food industry's total emissions and 26% of global greenhouse gas emissions. If this part of the food industry were a country, it would be the second largest emitter in the world, 26% being just a step behind emissions-leading China at 28% and far ahead of the next largest emitter, the US, at 15%.[118]

Having changed focus, Oatly launched a campaign called 'Flush the Milk' (Spola Mjölken), in reference to a Swedish government campaign from the 70s and 80s – 'Flush the Brandy' – that encouraged Swedes to drink less and exercise more.[119] The main message of the 'Flush the Milk' campaign was simple: if you switch from cow's milk to oat milk, you'll reduce greenhouse gas emissions by 75%. The campaign didn't hit a home run, neither with consumers nor with some of the farmers who supply Oatly. Farmers didn't appreciate the campaign because they think the agricultural sector is being unnecessarily targeted by the climate discussion while consumers thought the link to alcohol was inappropriate. Two weeks later, Arla's response was ready and they launched a new version of their 'Only milk tastes like milk' campaign.

Oatly has become available in various European countries since then. Even though they were legally precluded from using the slogan 'Just like milk, but made for humans' in Sweden, they were allowed to use it in other countries. In the UK, they launched the 'Ditch Milk' campaign (see figure 36). The poster claimed that switching to oat milk would save 73% in CO_2 emissions, but they were forced to stop the campaign because ASA, the government watchdog that previously blocked Shell, concluded that the claim was greenwashing due to the lack of specificity.

According to Oatly, it was all worth it. For them, it was about challenging the social norm and positioning themselves as part of the solution. Although they started out as a lactose-free alternative to milk, today they want to fuel the climate debate in every market they operate in. They want to make it clear to everyone how big an impact cow's milk has on the climate, an impact that is unnecessary. People can manage perfectly well without milk and if they do want something like milk, there are plenty of plant-based alternatives out there that have a much smaller climate impact. The company has showed no signs of letting up. It now also sells canned coffee drinks, dairy-free ice cream and vegan custard. Oatly sells its products in the US, UK, Australia, Croatia, China, South Korea, Italy, Singapore and Czechia.

FIGURE 36

Oatly's Ditch Milk advert in the UK

In 1968, biologist Paul Ehrlich published the book *The Population Bomb*. In it, he bluntly predicted that hundreds of millions of people would starve in the subsequent decade and that the growth of humankind had to be urgently brought under control. Today we know that there was no mass starvation of humankind. Ehrlich wrote his book a few years after global birth rates peaked and reached close to their peak in the global South. However, he was not alone; other futurists were also worried about population growth. They predicted a shortage of proteins needed to feed people, saying that not enough animals could be bred to provide the growing population with enough protein between 1980 and 1990. Lord Joseph Arthur Rank, a British industrialist, tasked his scientists with finding a non-animal solution to this potential problem. After evaluating more than 3,000 soil samples from around the world, they detected a micro-organism in the fungus family, called Fusarium venenatum, in 1967. They discovered a way to grow this fungus, ferment it and add it to mycoprotein; this was then dried and processed to take on the characteristics of meat. This protein option was brought to the market as Quorn in 1985. Nevertheless, in the end there was no protein shortage in the 80s. What Rank had envisioned as a complement to meat was not seen that way by the wider public. Quorn was thus dubbed a meat replacement, something exclusively designed for vegetarians.

FIGURE 37

Babies are trending (down)

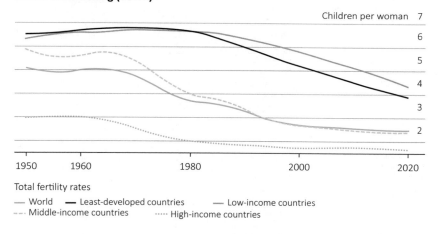

Total fertility rates

— World — Least-developed countries — Low-income countries
--- Middle-income countries ····· High-income countries

Today the situation has changed. Meat has become a real problem, not because we don't have enough of it, but because it has too much of a negative impact on the climate and biodiversity (see figure 38).

Food production as a whole is responsible for 17.3 billion tonnes of greenhouse gas emissions every year. That's more than double the entire emissions of the US and represents 35% of emissions worldwide. Meat is at the top of the emissions pyramid, responsible for almost 60% of all greenhouse gases emitted by food production, which is roughly equivalent to driving and flying all the cars, lorries and planes in the world.[120] And for what? At the moment, 83% of agricultural land is used for livestock and the crops they need for feed, but the meat and dairy products they produce only represent 18% of the calories consumed by people.[121] It doesn't seem to be very calorie-efficient.

FIGURE 38

Carbon footprint of different food products

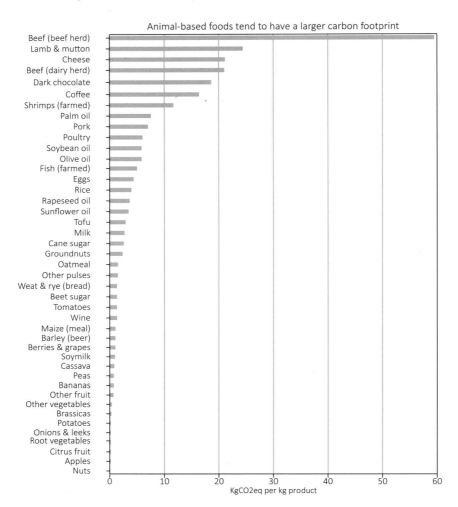

The impact on biodiversity is also staggering. The meat industry is the primary cause of deforestation worldwide and meat production causes twice as much pollution globally as the production of plant-based food.[122] Naturally, plant-based food also has a negative impact on the climate, but it's smaller – plant-based food products are responsible for 29% of emissions from food production.

Quorn's carbon footprint is ten times smaller than that of beef and four times smaller than that of chicken. Quorn uses 20 times less water than beef and six times less water than chicken. What used to be the greatest downside of Quorn, namely the idea that it was merely a meat replacement, has now become its greatest advantage. The British broadsheet newspaper, The Guardian, even wrote: "Replacing 20% of the world's beef consumption with microbial protein, such as Quorn, could halve the destruction of the planet's forests over the next three decades, according to the latest analysis."[123]

Three in ten British people say they are reducing their meat consumption.[124] While 14% say they don't eat any meat at all any more, 45% say they are flexitarian.[125] That represents an ideal opportunity for Quorn. But to make the most of it, the brand needs to shed the perception that it is a meat replacement, because it has a negative connotation. How can you turn things around to turn it into a positive choice? That's what the company is aiming to do with their 2021 campaign which positioned Quorn as the choice to make to have a positive impact on the climate. Solving the climate crisis is a gargantuan task. They don't want to give consumers the impression that it's up to them to solve it or to feel guilty about it; that is to say, they don't want to create any additional barriers. They want to give customers something which will help them make a step in the right direction: 'Helping the planet, one bite at a time' became the new campaign platform. They also don't want to come across as climate activists, which could scare away the greater public, but instead add a touch of necessary playfulness. In addition, they want to show the wider public how many, or few, CO_2 emissions are generated by their products. They've even put it on their packaging; figure 39 shows how much CO_2 is emitted per 1.3kg of Quorn Mince.

FIGURE 39

Quorn carbon-footprint label on pack

Quorn's positioning as part of the solution seems to be the right move for the company. Sales are rising and emissions are falling. In only eight weeks, eating Quorn instead of meat has prevented 3.8 million kg of CO_2 from being emitted into the atmosphere. That is the equivalent of driving more than 47.3 million kilometres in a petrol car, the water used by more than 89.4 million people in one day and enough energy to make 71.4 million cups of tea.[126] It seems like a gimmick to depict the results of brand repositioning with the number of CO_2 emissions that were prevented, but it's not. There's even a term for it: 'Avoided Emissions'. This term encompasses CO_2 emissions that were avoided thanks to the use of a certain product rather than the alternative with higher emissions. The climate community is not yet sure what the exact definition is or how exactly it should be measured, but it does align with the three scopes. Some people think that scope 4 is a better description than 'Avoided Emissions'. When we figure out what we should name it or how we should measure it, it will be a further opportunity for brands that are part of the solution to show how well they perform compared to companies that are still part of the problem.

Both Quorn and Oatly are brands that didn't set out to solve the climate problem with their product, but that had the solution right there in front of them. The better our understanding of the climate crisis becomes, the more valuable that 'hidden' solution will be. Really, hidden or not, they're also already part of the solution. They stand alongside the New Climate-Friendly companies, but also the Traditional Climate-Friendly companies.

The 'traditional' climate-friendly companies

"Patagonia's CEO flies to Albania to support the campaign to save the Vjosa river," appears on your timeline. You have no idea what's going on, but if Patagonia is getting involved, it must be important. Patagonia is a company you can trust. You choose their clothes because they keep up with the latest fashion trends, but mostly because they're high-quality and climate-friendly. You know that your money is not being put towards a shareholder's super yacht, but towards projects that protect nature and the climate. Many stories have already confirmed this. All the money Patagonia earned on Black Friday in 2017 was donated to nature groups they support. They did the same with the money they saved thanks to President Trump's tax cuts in 2019. The company says on its website 'We are in business to save the home planet' and you know that statement isn't just mumbo jumbo. When you then read that Ryan

Gellert flew to Albania to support a river project, that can only be good news for the project.

The Vjosa river is the last untouched and unspoiled wild river in Europe. It stretches across more than 270 kilometres, from Greece to the Adriatic Sea. It is the lifeline of many Albanian communities that live along its banks. The Albanian government had plans to build eight large dams, 30 smaller dams and a hydropower plant. They wanted to use the river to produce green energy, but that would have meant that the river would lose its natural uniqueness and that its ecosystem, with 1,100 species living in the river, including 140 which are protected under Albanian law, would be damaged. Moreover, roughly 40 species are on the international list of endangered species. It also meant that many villages would disappear and residents would be displaced. The people weren't in favour of this project – in fact, 93% of Albanians were against it – and that's not to mention various international environment organisations and a group of scientists. They wanted the area around the river to become a designated national park, the first 'wild river national park' in Europe, and thus gain protected status. Among the Albanian population, 94% thought this was a good idea and Patagonia decided to back them. It made a short documentary calling on the local population to make their voice heard in the elections on 25th April 2021 and appealing to the international community to make the protest resonate throughout the world.

When he arrived in Albania, Ryan Gellert bluntly voiced his opinion: "Hydropower plants are not green, not sustainable, not cost-efficient, and are sending species to extinction and displacing populations." He personally called on the Albanian people to put pressure on politicians. The efforts of environmental organisations, scientists and Patagonia all bore their fruit. In January 2022, the government attributed the status of 'natural park' to the area round the river and on 13th June 2022 it definitively became a 'national park'. The danger for people, animals and climate had thus passed.

Where did this steadfast belief come from? Why did the CEO step on a plane to go and plead a climate case on the other side of the world? Why does the CEO publicly state that consumers urgently have to consume less and, yes, that includes his brand's clothing? Why is Patagonia going to such lengths to help their customers wear their clothes for longer, asking customers to bring clothes they no longer wear back so they can be repaired and sold second-hand? It's a B Corporation, but that can't be the whole story. I asked

Ryan Gellert all of these questions while the documentary *The Decade of Action* was being filmed. His answer? Yvon Chouinard, founder and owner of Patagonia, is a billionaire climate activist who, in his book *Let my people go surfing*, wrote that if you want to understand an entrepreneur, you have to understand their younger self: "If you want to understand the entrepreneur, study the juvenile delinquent. The delinquent is saying with his actions: This sucks. I'm going to do my own thing." Let's try doing what he says.

In the middle of the last century, a young Yvon Chouinard became a member of the Southern California Falconry Club, where he developed a passion for rock climbing. In 1957, when he was 18 years old, he learned how to make his own rock climbing equipment. He bought a second-hand smithy and taught himself how to forge. He made his first pitons, spikes that climbers drive into crevices, with steel and sold them for $1.50 a piece to other climbers. He started doing good business quickly, so good, in fact, that Chouinard Equipment became the largest supplier of climbing gear in the US by 1970.

But there was a problem. The company's equipment was damaging rocks. Given that climbing trails are often repetitively used by different people and that those pins are driven and hammered into the same fragile crevices, the damage to mountains just kept getting worse. After a while, Chouinard thought, this practice could endanger the sport. Together with his business partner, Tom Frost, they decided to stop producing the steel pins, despite the fact that they represented 70% of the company's revenue. Chouinard subsequently introduced an alternative: aluminium clamps that could be wedged tight by hand and thus caused a lot less damage to the rocks. They were launched in the company's first catalogue in 1972, to which Chouinard wrote the introduction himself. His words speak to his true motivations. To understand why Patagonia does what it does and why it will only become more successful, you just need to read that short text. It reads like a climate leaflet today.

"No longer can we assume the Earth's resources are limitless; that there are ranges of unclimbed peaks extending endlessly beyond the horizon. Mountains are finite, and despite their massive appearance, they are fragile...We believe the only way to ensure the climbing experience for ourselves and future generations is to preserve (1) the vertical wilderness, and (2) the adventure inherent in the experience. Really, the only insurance to guarantee this adventure and the safest insurance to maintain it, is exercise of moral restraint and individual responsibility.

Thus, it is the style of the climb, not attainment of the summit, which is the measure of personal success. Traditionally stated, each of us must consider whether the end is more important than the means. Given the vital importance of style we suggest that the keynote is simplicity. The fewer gadgets between the climber and the climb, the greater is the chance to attain the desired communication with oneself—and nature. The equipment offered in this catalogue attempts to support this ethic."[127]

FIGURE 40

Patagonia's mission statement

He called it 'clean climbing' and it changed the sport for good. The catalogue became the bible for a new style of climbing that climbers are still thankful for today. What would be left of the rocks had we continued to climb as we did 70 years ago, they wonder. Here speaks a man with a mission, a mission that is much more important than his business success. He couldn't accept his business being part of the problem, even if that problem represented 70% of their revenue stream. So he solved the problem. In the meantime, Chouinard also developed a clothing business. During a winter climbing trip to Scotland, he bought a rugby shirt that he then wore for climbing. It had a collar to make sure that the hardware slings didn't cut into his neck. Once he was back in America, Chouinard kept wearing the shirt to climb which made his climbing friends also want one. The shirts quickly became a small fashion trend in the United States so the company decided to separate the clothing division under a different name: Patagonia. The mission, however, remained the same: doing business with the greatest respect for the outdoors and the conservation thereof so that future generations could also enjoy it.

"We are in business to save the home planet." That's how Patagonia rephrased its mission a few years ago (see figure 40). For Chouinard, these are not just words. On 14th September 2022, he announced that he, and his family, would be donating all of their shares in Patagonia – valued at around $3 billion – to a trust and non-profit organisation specifically created for the purpose, set up to safeguard the company's autonomy and ensure that all profits – some $100 million a year – are spent on fighting climate change and protecting land around the world. The Earth thus became Patagonia's sole shareholder, in the final implementation of Chouinard's vision.

"Before we look at the numbers, we'd like to know what kind of positive impact your company will have with this project." Greo Belgers, Group Marketing Director, told me that you will be asked this question if you apply for a business loan with Triodos. Triodos is a bank, but different. It's a sustainable bank. The first. The real thing. That's why they want to know precisely how a company will contribute to making the world more sustainable before it even thinks about issuing a loan. For them, their clients using that money for projects that would make the world less sustainable is unthinkable.

It all started in 1968 when economist Adriaan Deking Dura, professor Dieter Brüll, management consultant Lex Bos and banker Rudolf Mees set up a study group to find an answer to the question of how you can make the world more sustainable by putting money in the right places. They founded the bank, Triodos, in 1980. Seven years later, the bank had its first watershed moment. "The year 1987 was an important year in the history of Triodos Bank," explains Belgers. "It was the year after the Chernobyl disaster. The importance of climate-friendly energy was growing. Triodos believed that building wind farms was critical and wanted to make loans available for this purpose. However, there were no wind farms to fund – it was still too early – so we decided to do it ourselves." Peter Blom, who later became CEO of Triodos, travelled through the Netherlands to convince local authorities of their plan together with a wind farm developer. They succeeded, with Triodos becoming the first backer of one of the most prominent changes in the energy landscape while other banks continued to focus elsewhere. The risk profile of a windmill farm was still too high for many but Triodos wasn't doing it for the money – only later did it become a major income stream for the bank. For them, it was about making the first step toward a change they deemed crucial to make society more sustainable. They couldn't do that in all sectors, which is why they selected a few areas to focus on, areas in which they absolutely wanted to bring about change: energy and climate, food and agriculture, and social inclusion.

In 2015, Triodos was the first pan-European bank to become a B Corporation. In 2018, it was the first bank in the world to publish a report on the carbon footprint of its loan and investment portfolios. In the meantime, Triodos has become a climate-neutral organisation. It measures the footprint of its activities and completely offsets it with Gold Standard projects by the Climate Neutral group. At the end of 2021, they shared their climate plan stating that they will reach their net-zero target by 2035. All three scopes are being taken into account, which includes the emissions produced by all loans and investments. That's a massive undertaking for a bank. Since then, almost all banks are calling themselves sustainable which encourages Greo Belgers: "The more banks invest money and issue loans to companies with projects that make the world more sustainable, the faster we'll succeed. That's a positive change." However, he is worried about banks that continue to invest in the fossil-fuel industry. "The IPCC was clear. The tap must close now if we want a chance of not exceeding 1.5 degrees."

For years, Triodos has been the steady, sustainable face of the financial sector. Most other banks are in a transition phase, trying to build up a green portfolio while dismantling their brown portfolio. But that sometimes goes wrong.

On 31st May 2022, German police raided the offices of DWS and its majority shareholder, Deutsche Bank. DWS is the asset manager of Deutsche Bank. The raid was part of an investigation into greenwashing allegations. It seemed that, in their 2020 annual report, DWS had stated that more than half of their managed assets were invested in ESG-certified funds and companies.[128] A whistle-blower raised serious objections to this claim. It was said that DWS had loosely interpreted ESG criteria and was merely using it as a marketing tool. Apparently, they had nowhere near that many investments that were worthy of the ESG name. Since then, evidence has backed these greenwashing claims. In March 2022, they reported that in 2021 they had 115 billion euros invested in an 'ESG-asset' portfolio, when just one year earlier they had claimed to have 548 billion euros invested in 'ESG-integrated' assets.

ESG stands for environmental, social and governance; it's represented with a score. The more you fulfil ESG criteria, the higher your score. The aim is to ensure that the world's capital is invested in companies with a high ESG score, because this means that invested capital is being used to make the world more sustainable. ESG has not lost any momentum in recent years. Nearly 3 trillion dollars are invested in ESG funds, predominantly in Europe (see figure 41).[129]

FIGURE 41

The global rise of ESG funds

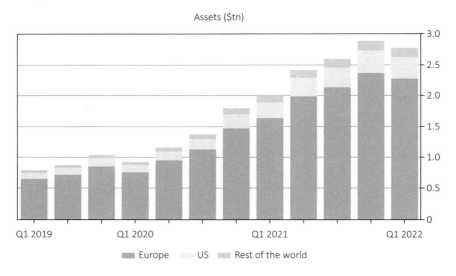

Assets ($tn)

Q1 2019   Q1 2020   Q1 2021   Q1 2022

■ Europe   US   ■ Rest of the world

However, an ESG score is subjective. There are no globally accepted criteria for it, which means that it does raise some controversy. On 18th May 2022, S&P Global removed Tesla from an ESG index, replacing it with Exxon Mobil. Tesla is often praised for it's high 'E' credentials because it manufactured three-quarters of the new electric cars produced last year in the US. Nevertheless, the minerals used to make these cars sometimes come from dirty mines that entail poor working conditions. In addition, Tesla has been criticised for the poor working conditions in its own factories. As a result, S&P Global decided it scored high for E but low for S, thus removing it from their index. The market reacted quickly and Tesla's market price fell by 6%. This was no laughing matter for Elon Musk. He couldn't stand his company, which is obviously part of the solution, being replaced by a fossil-fuel company that couldn't be any further from being part of the solution. On Twitter, he wrote: "ESG is a scam. It has been weaponised by phony social justice warriors."[130]

Musk is not the only one who shares this opinion. "It creates a dangerous placebo that damages the overall importance," explains Tariq Fancy.[131] Fancy was an adviser to the department of sustainable investments at BlackRock, the world's largest asset manager and a champion of sustainable investments. In his opinion, an ESG certificate is a smoke screen; too many companies score well even though they have absolutely no intention of making the world a better place. To further highlight this issue, on 11th June 2022 the Financial Times reported that the American Securities and Exchange Commission (SEC) had launched an investigation into the asset management department at Goldman Sachs and the ESG claims they had made.[132] The turmoil around ESG has been going on for a while and shows that stricter rules are needed in order for such a system to work well. That's why new accounting standards are in the process of being drawn up, by the International Sustainability Standards Board (ISSB), to create the same transparency for a company's ESG results as for their financial results. Even policy makers are seeking stronger regulations about what ESG does or doesn't mean and how it should be measured.

The idea behind ESG scores is strong and valuable, just like the idea behind net-zero. If properly applied, it could bring about the change we need. For the business sector, these two tools show whether a company is part of the solution or not, which means that companies can use them to tackle their credibility deficit. That's exactly why they're used as a marketing and PR tool but, as we've seen, this can sometimes go wrong. What's worse, ESG chaos was to be expected; many parties had already warned us that it might backfire. In February 2022, the Financial Times wrote: "Industry insiders are starting to worry that some of the overly optimistic or misleading ESG claims that have been made in fund documents and marketing could trigger a mis-selling scandal similar to those in diesel cars."[133] The alarm bells must be sounding now, because a situation like this would certainly augment transition risks. In the case of DWS, it will take them some time to recover from the damage to their reputation. Policy makers are now even more convinced that they need to implement regulatory measures quickly, while the majority of investors will be much more cynical when someone advises them to increase their investments in ESG funds. Why would a company like DWS, that called itself "one of the world's leading asset managers with 902 billion euros of assets under management", be so casual with their ESG credentials?[134] If you're that high-profile, why would you risk getting caught? In order to understand, we need to go back to 1970 to a newspaper article published in the New York Times.

Milton Friedman defined his Friedman doctrine in an article published in the New York Times under the headline: 'The Social Responsibility Of Business Is to Increase Its Profits'.[135] He maintained that a company's only task, and definitely the only task for the company's management, was to create as much profit as possible for its shareholders within the legal and ethical framework of the society in which the company operates. According to Friedman, there were limits to that social responsibility. He believed that companies weren't responsible for the negative externalities caused by their business, but were the responsibility of the government. Externalities are effects caused by the business operations of a company on a third party. Electricity, for example, is generated by a producer and sold to a consumer, but CO_2 is released when generating that electricity, thus having a negative effect on climate change. This creates a negative externality which, under Friedman's logic, is a task for the government.

Friedman published his first shareholder statement in a time when the digital transparency of today didn't exist, but powerful authorities did. He believed that society's strenuous problems, like pollution, were better left to the government because they were the only party with the power necessary to take it on. At that time, 25 years after the Second World War, the government was still seen as an effective entity. Environmental activists like Rachel Carson, who was fighting to ban pesticides like DDT, preferred to work with politicians and unions, avoiding business leaders and investors.

Today we have digital transparency but a lot less confidence in the ability of governments to solve problems. Belgians are doing the same as the rest of the world, they're looking to companies to solve current issues. Whether business leaders like it or not, they are expected to influence policy and even to tackle the problem themselves. Companies that don't do this are more often than not seen as part of the problem. Companies that do take the lead are gaining credibility as part of the solution. That's why some CEOs are very tempted to tell the world exactly what their company is doing to become part of the solution. John Gapper from the Financial Times puts it as follows: "Meeting financial targets is tedious but promising to save the world sounds heroic."[136] This trend is like the transition to the Anthropocene, in that what's done is done. The clearer the negative impact of the climate crisis becomes, the louder the call for the business sector to take social leadership will get. Triodos and Patagonia are companies that have social climate leadership in their DNA. They should remain as they are, because who they are is a more and more valuable asset.

Of course, there are other companies built on values of ethical leadership. Unilever, Cadbury, Quaker, Clarks, Danone and The Body Shop are all companies whose founders were driven by a strong set of social and ethical values. It's no surprise that mammoth organisations like Danone and Unilever are taking the lead on climate among multinationals. However, we can't call them traditional climate-friendly companies because their historical footprint is just too big.

THE CLIMATE BARRIER NO-ONE IS TALKING ABOUT

I have a question for you: How often did you doubt what you were reading earlier about climate friendliness and climate-friendly companies? When you were reading Dash Water's story, some of you surely thought that a drink sold in an aluminium can couldn't be all that climate-friendly. When you were reading the Tru Earth detergent story, you were probably raising your eyebrows. While reading this book, some readers have most likely felt the word 'greenwashing' bubbling up inside them on more than one occasion. Am I right?

Consumer doubts about whether a company truly is climate-friendly or whether they're doing it out of need or as a marketing ploy are deeply rooted. Friedman may have died in 2006, but his train of thought has had a lasting impact on business leadership strategies and how consumers think about companies. Consequently, those doubts are still there. And just when people start thinking that things will be different, another Dieselgate emerges. Consumers have a short memory span. The names of questionable companies may disappear from their minds, but that overall cynicism sticks around and rears its head every time a company mentions being climate-friendly, sustainability, 'being a force for good' or 'doing well by doing good'. Only companies like Patagonia and Triodos can escape that trap, but they're also twice as old as their youngest customers. They've proven enough times that they don't live in the world as Friedman saw it.

Those doubts that lay dormant in consumers and lead to disbelief and distrust at every opportunity are the climate risk that no-one is talking about. Moreover, those misgivings intensify whenever a consumer is personally affected by the negative impact of the climate crisis. There are three reasons for this:

1. As we've mentioned a few times now, consumers want companies to take the lead. First of all, the business sector is seen as the only party that has the knowledge, the leadership and the money under their belt to safely lead us through the sustainability transition. Secondly, they reason that it's also in the best interest of companies; the business sector can't save itself if the climate has not been stabilised.

2. Despite the best efforts of the business sector, consumers today don't feel like the business sector is doing enough. If you ask them, they are still wholly unsatisfied. More than 80% of Belgians say that they don't see enough climate action being taken by businesses. Of course, consumers don't know what is going on behind the scenes, but when it comes to external results, the consensus among consumers is clear: much too LITTLE is being done.

3. The third reason is down to businesses themselves: companies greenwash. Or is that greenwishing? Whatever it may be, consumers consider that 59% of the sustainability campaigns they have seen over the last two years in Belgium are greenwashing.

Let's recap. Consumers want the business sector to take leadership, but they don't see much action being taken and if action is taken, six times out of ten they think it's greenwashing. Are we still surprised that we are facing a credibility deficit? What about the fact that only 13% of consumers think that multinationals are being honest when they explain how they will make the world a better place (see figure 44)? That even the most climate-friendly companies can convince only a fifth of consumers that they are being sincere? That can't be right.

This is the critical climate barrier no-one is talking about, because we simply don't think it exists. As marketers and advertising professionals, we have never needed to pay so much attention to our credibility. We promised cleaning products that would make a disgusting, greasy kitchen counter sparkling clean in just one wipe. We promised washing-up liquids that would make dishes we thought we'd never get completely clean sparkling clean in just one quick wash. We promised toothpaste that would make our teeth sparkling white after the first brush and electric cars that can drive distances of 500 km

SIX TIMES OUT OF TEN CONSUMERS THINK IT'S GREENWASHING

---

in the advert but only 400 in practice. No consumer ever came to ask for their money back the next day when it turned out these claims weren't true. For consumers, they were just adverts.

Nevertheless, when it comes to the future of our planet, everything changes. When talking about the planet, every word counts. It's not just about what we're doing, but also about the intention behind those actions. In this world, a company's credibility is key to successfully becoming part of the solution, to separating the wheat from the chaff and setting that moral compass true North. Lack of credibility is why consumers won't want to try another brand or even want anything to do with them. Just like those doubts, the value of credibility will continue to grow as the negative impacts of the climate crisis increase.

FIGURE 42

Credibility score of campaigns across sectors (%)

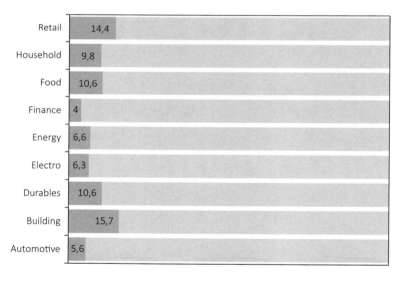

How can a company become more credible? Through what it says, does and is. Doing and being is binary; either you're climate-friendly or you're not. It shows through in what you do or don't do. However, what you say about what you're doing is where you can portray your actions to consumers; your words are how you show them that you are part of the solution. That's where the snag lies, as you can see in figure 42. Not one single sector has a good credibility score. Only 4% of campaigns from the financial sector are credible. The retail sector scores slightly better, but only 14% of its campaigns are credible (figure 42). There is visible variation; some sectors are doing slightly better than others, but the overall outcome is quite negative. These results point to a language issue. We're not speaking the right language; the way in which we are talking about the climate is not credible to the consumer. That's normal. After all, companies speak to convince: choose me, not them. But how can you convince someone who, before you've even started your story, says that they don't believe a single word? You can't, can you?

Companies need to talk about climate friendliness. The question is what kind of language they should use to do that. Professor Gino Verleye, from the University of Ghent, Inez Schoenaers, from Bubka, and I researched this issue and the results are clear: the language of the climate normal sounds different. It's important that we, in the business sector, learn to speak that language because consumers are asking brands and companies to speak up and to do it now. The learning curve is going to be steep.

The Amazon lost 17% from its forest

THE GREAT HESITATION IN NUMBERS

Biodiversity Loss Today

Since 1955, the alteration of biodiversity related to human activities has been greater than any other time in human history.

! Over 12,000 species are threatened with extinction.

+12.000 species are threatened

! One-third of the world's coral reefs have died off.

! As of 2021, just 9% of the world's forests remain intact.

! The Amazon has already lost 17% of its forest cover and an additional 17% of its rainforests have been degraded.

! Only 3% of the world's oceans are free from human pressures.

! Europe is home to the highest proportion of species under threat of extinction.

! The 2019-2020 Australian bushfires are estimated to have killed nearly 3 billion native vertebrates.

! Genetic diversity within breeds is declining, and 17% of the 8,774 livestock breeds identified are classified as at risk of disappearing.

! Between 1900-2000, roughly 75% of the genetic diversity of agricultural crops was lost.

5 mass extinctions in Earth's history

! In Earth's history, there have been five mass extinctions, defined as time periods where extinction rates accelerate relative to origination rates such that over 75% of species disappear over an interval of 2 million years or less. Current extinction rates are higher than those leading to the five mass extinctions.

Sources

TRVST. (2022, 31 May). *Biodiversity Facts & Statistics*. Last accessed on 4 June 2022, at https://www.trvst.world/biodiversity/biodiversity-facts-statistics/

Facts About the Loss of Biodiversity. (n.d.). chillingfacts.org.uk. Last accessed on 4 June 2022, at https://www.chillingfacts.org.uk/facts-about-the-loss-of-biodiversity.html

Greenpeace International. (n.d.). *10 facts about biodiversity, nature protection, and Indigenous Peoples' rights*. Last accessed on 4 June 2022, at https://www.greenpeace.org/international/story/53918/10-facts-biodiversity-nature-protection-indigenous-peoples-rights/

Speak Up Now.

 For silence is doing nothing.
Danielle Lucia Schaffer

WORDS MATTER

Thanks to language, we can share experiences, learn from each other, talk to each other and make plans for the future, often in the form of long or short stories. These stories are important; they are some of the oldest forms of communication. From telling stories around a campfire to catching up on the latest TV series, people love consuming stories. They serve to relax us, but also to pass on knowledge and information. Stories have a profound impact on our culture because they give it shape, like a blueprint that determines what behaviour is good or bad, desirable or undesirable, socially acceptable or socially unacceptable. Story-telling also helps us to evolve, helping us see that discrimination based on skin colour is not acceptable, that human trafficking must stop and that minority groups deserve equal rights. Stories also outline our future, by telling the story of where we want to go, of what is feasible or not.

Given that they reach people on every level – not just their head, but also their emotions, values and imagination – it's important that the blueprint of our future be inspiring and motivating. Russia's invasion of Ukraine is an example of how powerful stories can be and how they determine how we think about the future. At first, the overall expectation was that one of the most powerful militaries in the world would take control of Ukraine in no time. However, once that first day ended, it was already clear that it wouldn't be so easy. We heard stories of courageous Ukrainians who stood in front of Russian tanks, unarmed. We heard the story of 13 soldiers on Snake Island who, in response to a Russian assault vessel's request for them to surrender, answered: "Russian warship, go fuck yourself."[137] We heard President Zelensky's answer to the US offer to evacuate him: "I need ammo, not a ride."[138] These are now iconic stories that have not only given form to the vague images we had in our minds of Ukrainians, but have also given them hope that they can beat the Russians.

Advertising campaigns are short stories that, at times, can have a very large impact. Our image of female beauty is changing, partly thanks to Dove's stories. The idea that our clothing should become more climate-friendly, meanwhile, is partly down to Patagonia's stories. More than 600 billion dollars is spent on advertising every year. That is enough to have a positive influence on the story that is told about the climate transition. The words we use to do that are far more important than we might think.

Recent research shows that the way in which a language's grammar marks the future has an impact on both individual climate-friendly behaviour and national climate-friendly policies.[139] Some languages, like Finnish, don't have a dedicated future tense. Instead of saying "Tomorrow, we will go to the cinema", they talk about tomorrow as if it were today: "Tomorrow, we go to the cinema". Finnish speakers make tomorrow's activities sound as if they're an absolute certainty. In English, Dutch, French and many other languages, however, there is a future tense. In those languages, using the future tense – i.e. "We will go to the cinema tomorrow" – means that it's likely to happen but is not fully certain yet, there's still a possibility things might change.

Whether a language has a future tense or not seems to have an impact on the willingness to act and climate friendliness of people and communities as a whole. According to the scientific report, someone who speaks a language which uses a future tense is 20% less inclined to help protect the environment than someone speaking in the present tense, while 24% are also less willing to pay higher taxes for climate-friendly policies. Researchers have noticed the same trend on a national level. Countries with a more 'present-day language' tend to have stricter climate policies. The researchers thus concluded that speaking about the future as if it were today makes the climate issue feel much closer. People are more concerned about things that affect them directly, so people who speak a language with weak future-tense markers are more likely to adopt more climate-friendly behaviour more quickly. This shows that words are important. Words have an impact on a consumer's willingness to act on the climate and even the willingness of an entire country.

Consequently, it is vital that companies speak the right language. The advertising lingo we currently speak is the language of the old normal, it's the language of the Mad Men who reinvented advertising in the 1960s, last century. Using that language in the new climate normal doesn't work. A tweet in response to a Dutch KLM campaign, explaining that it is possible to fly in a 'climate-friendly' way, made this quite clear: "What goes on in the mind of marketing people who forge the way for companies to psychologically manipulate us into perpetrating ecocide for short-term profit?"[140]

A different language is spoken in the new climate normal and we are being called on from two sides to choose our words wisely. Firstly, the government wants to prevent consumers being given misleading information. They're asking us to adapt our language to make it more accurate, more detailed and less open to interpretation. Consumers also have different expectations in the new climate normal concerning how we talk to them about climate friendliness. They expect more transparency and more commitment. They want to know that we understand solutions are urgently needed and they want details that clearly show that the solutions we're offering are valuable. Companies that are part of the solution take these expectations seriously and are adapting to the new climate normal. Let us delve further into what governments and consumers are truly asking of us.

HOW GOVERNMENTS ARE ASKING US TO ADAPT OUR LANGUAGE

Zoe is a young woman, sitting on the sofa and watching TV. There is a burger on the coffee table in front of her, waiting to be devoured. A man's voice, reminiscent of a documentary producer, says: "The planet is continuing to warm". A woman's voice answers: "Now that's not what Zoe likes to hear." With a worried look in her eye, Zoe grabs the ketchup bottle and squeezes some onto her burger. "But she's gonna roll up her sleeves and do her bit." Zoe rolls up her sleeves. "Told you," says the voice. Zoe drags the coffee table closer, grabs her burger and takes a big bite. "And there it is, a delicious Tesco

Plant Chef burger. We've lowered the price of dozens of our Plant Chef products because a little swap can make a big difference to the planet." The ad
ends with: "Tesco, every little helps".

At first sight, there doesn't seem to be anything wrong with this ad. They're
saying that a plant-based burger is better for the climate than a meat burger.
We all know that plant-based food is better for the climate than meat, so it
doesn't seem like Tesco did anything wrong. However, that's not what the
Advertising Standards Authority (ASA) thought. The ASA is the independent watchdog for advertisements in the UK. If consumers have complaints
about an advert, they can submit their complaint to the ASA that will then
examine whether the campaign complies with the advertising standards
established by the Committees of Advertising Practice (CAP). This particular
ad campaign received 171 consumer complaints. After conducting an investigation, the ASA concluded that the ad implies that switching to products
from the Plant Chef range would have a positive impact on the climate. They
thus expected proof that this was the case across the complete life cycle of
a Plant Chef burger compared to a meat burger. The report said: "However,
we understood that Tesco did not hold any evidence in relation to the full life
cycle of any of the products in the Plant Chef range, or of the burger featured
in the ads. We were therefore unable to assess the product's total environment impact over its life cycle compared with that of a meat burger. Because
we had not seen evidence that demonstrated that Plant Chef products could
make a positive environmental difference to the planet compared to their
meat equivalents, nor had we seen evidence for the full life cycle of the Plant
Chef burger, we concluded the claims regarding their positive benefits to the
planet had not been substantiated and were likely to mislead."[141] Tesco's ad
was thus banned. The day after the decision was published, the headline of
the Financial Times read: "Tesco rebuked over greenwashing in adverts for
plant-based food."[142] Other media soon followed suit. 7th June 2022 was not
a great day for Tesco, because all media channels were telling consumers that
it was greenwashing.

This is the perfect example of how our language must change. In the old
normal, this ad explains clearly and simply that if you opt for a plant-based
burger, you are making a positive choice for the climate. It adds that you
can find this environmental benefit in Tesco Plant Chef burgers for a cheaper
price. In the new normal, however, these claims are seen as greenwashing
and you're thus forbidden from using that ad, because the information that

is needed to back that climate promise is not readily available. It's all about a lack of proof. However, due to all the media attention that this case generated, consumers are under the impression that Tesco is only telling half-truths and is not to be believed. This obviously does nothing to help your cause, even if you are making every effort to be seen as a company that is part of the solution in the eyes of consumers. Worst of all, this could have been avoided; the UK's business sector was warned that this kind of crackdown was coming. On 20th September 2021, the CMA (Competitions and Markets Authority) issued an official warning to the British business sector that by the end of 2021, all sustainable marketing claims must abide by the definitions set out in the new Green Claims Code.

FIGURE 43

Green claims code in the UK

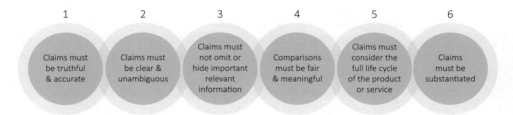

If adverts don't abide by this code, harsh penalties will be imposed. The list of campaigns that they have since banned following consumer complaints clearly shows that the British authorities are keeping their word. Companies and brands such as Oatly, Innocent, Hyundai, Ryanair, Quorn, Pepsi, Lipton and Shell have already fallen foul of the code.[143] According to the ASA, marketers urgently need to adapt their language when talking about being climate-friendly: "In too many cases we're seeing examples where advertisers over-claim or where claims lack precision. And too often we hear the defence that the advertiser had intended to say something else. We don't regulate ads on the basis of an advertiser's intentions, though."[144] In April 2022, Innocent – who had just had one of their campaigns banned – appealed to the British advertising industries and authorities to work together to clarify the new rules. Internally, it also implemented new measures by merging the marketing and sustainability departments. With this decision, they hope to ensure "clearer guidelines on greenwashing, which would stop marketers from being paralysed by the fear of being called out."[145] Innocent, a company that is doing its utmost to be seen as a climate-friendly company by consumers, is trying to avoid the term 'greenwasher' like the plague. Once tainted, the term hangs around for far too long.

This is an example of the transition risks that the climate crisis presents. In this case, policy makers are increasing the risk of reputational damage to brands if they do not abide by new policy rules. This kind of situation isn't unique to the UK. In early 2021, the EU investigated the sustainability claims made by European companies. The results did not paint a pretty picture: 59% of sustainability claims were considered to be greenwashing, as it seemed that they were not backed by sufficient evidence.[146] In some cases, companies even create their own 'eco-friendly' labels to put on their packaging, without explaining what criteria the product must fulfil in order to earn that label. There are also products dubbed 'CO_2-neutral' without any explanation as to what that term means exactly, nor what measures have been taken. But that's not all. In 42% of cases, claims seem to be misleading or, worse still, fake. That carries a lot more risk than one might think, because it contravenes the 'Unfair Commercial Practice EU Directive'. Violating this directive could land a company in court. After the report was published, it was clear that the EU had to strengthen the rules. The 'Environmental performance of products & businesses – substantiating claims' proposal, to be passed by the European Commission this year, defines the rules surrounding a company's climate-friendly claims, setting out which criteria they must fulfil and how that can be measured. Nevertheless, not all national governments are waiting for the EU's proposal to come into force. At the beginning of 2021, the Consumer & Market Authority (ACM) in the Netherlands published a series of strict guidelines that companies must abide by. If companies fail to do so, they will be asked to stop their advertising campaigns. France has gone a step further. If everything goes to plan, all advertising for fossil fuels will be banned by the end of 2022 and no more adverts for cars with a combustion engine will be allowed from 2028. In Belgium, new measures are also in the works.

It's obvious what policy makers' intentions are: Every climate promise made by a company must also come true. This is evaluated from the perspective of consumers, meaning that it's not about what a company wants to say, but about how the consumer interprets it. This means that we can't leave anything open to interpretation.

Climate claims must be accurate and clear

A company's promises must be correct. It seems strange to think that companies' promises could be wrong but really, in the new normal, 'correct' means that there can be no room for 'incorrect' interpretation by consumers. From the outset, a company has to ask itself whether its climate promise could potentially be interpreted in different ways. If so, that promise must be explained more clearly to remove any of that room for interpretation. Imagine a fashion brand that calls itself 'a sustainable brand' because it launched a collection of t-shirts made of organic cotton. That brand must thus ask itself whether consumers will be under the impression that all of its collections are sustainable, given that it calls itself 'a sustainable brand'. Consumers could interpret this terminology as proof that the brand as a whole, including all of its collections, is sustainable. If the company cannot prove that all its other collections are sustainable, the brand cannot make such a promise.

The same goes for a brand that promises that the production of all its goods will be carbon-neutral. If no more detail is given, this could create the impression that their products are manufactured with a carbon-emissions cut of 100%. If that is not the case, perhaps because some of those carbon emissions are offset by planting trees, it has to be explained to consumers. The company would be better off not making that carbon-neutral promise if it doesn't explain what it means by that to consumers. Generic climate promises such as 'environmentally-friendly' or 'natural' can also cause problems. Regulators will question what is meant exactly by those phrases and if that can be backed by evidence. If the claim remains vague, it will question whether consumers could interpret it more 'widely' than intended and perhaps take action as a result.

The same goes for companies promising that something is 'biodegradable', 'compostable' or 'recyclable'; that label must apply to the whole product and not just a part of it. This mistake was made by a trainer brand that included the phrase '50% recycled' in their adverts. According to the regulator, consumers could think that this applied to the whole trainer but, in reality, only the sole of the shoe was 50% recycled. The campaign was thus banned.

What about promoting net-zero plans? Most of these promises have a 30-year timeframe. Many companies don't even know exactly how they will implement their plan and if it's not yet clear for the company, how can they explain it clearly to consumers? A lot could happen between now and then; no company can guarantee that nothing will go wrong, that there won't be a delay, or some other impediment to their plan. The regulator is understanding about unknown situations putting a spanner in the works, but they're not lenient when it comes to what a net-zero plan actually means. If a company promotes their net-zero plan, they must also have a detailed and verifiable plan of implementation.

Climate promises are indivisible

Imagine soup sold in a carton with the slogan: 'Friend of nature – better for the environment'.[147] This wording could give consumers the impression that the claim is valid for both the packaging and the product. Is that true? The vegetables used to make the soup are indeed grown sustainably, but the packaging contains a layer of non-recyclable plastic. This means that the climate promise cannot be applied to the whole product and the regulator will ask the company to be more specific. The climate friendliness of a product is determined by several factors: the origin of the raw materials and components, the production processes used, as well as packaging, transport, use and processing after use. If a climate promise could give the impression that it is valid across the whole spectrum and the company can substantiate this claim, then there's no problem. However, if the product fails to live up to that promise on just one of those aspects, the claim must be made more specific so that the consumer clearly understands that it doesn't apply to all stages of the process.

Climate-based comparisons must be fair

Climate-friendly products are often promoted as being better for the climate than a regular product. If companies make this kind of comparison, they have to do so fairly. They must ensure they are comparing apples to apples, making a comparison that is clear, objective and up-to-date. If a toothbrush brand says that its new toothbrush contains 60% less plastic than other toothbrushes on the market, it must have compared that product to *all* the other toothbrushes on the market. However, if they only compared their product to a select group of toothbrushes, the company must clarify exactly which ones they're talking about. Furthermore, consumers must also be able to consult that data easily.

If searching for that data is more arduous than simply scanning a QR code or typing in a URL, the company may be asked to simplify the process. These rules apply whether you're comparing your sustainable products with products by another brand or with your own products (old versus new products, for example). You do not have more leeway just because you're comparing your new product to your other products. If a fashion brand releases a new range of shirts claiming to contain '50% more recycled fibres', the regulator is highly likely to question that claim and ask for clarification about which shirts the comparison applies to.

Climate friendliness always takes into account the full life cycle of a product

Most watchdogs require comparisons and claims to be based on the full life cycle of a product. The supporting data must also be easy to access. If a brand promotes a product with the climate promise '33% fewer carbon emissions', it must be crystal clear what exactly that means. We can expect consumers to interpret this as applying to the whole of the product's emissions, in other words, the entire life cycle of the product. If that's not the case, perhaps because scope 3 or transport is not included in the calculation, the climate promise must be refined.

All in all, those are the most important requirements that policy makers expect brands and companies to comply with when it comes to climate friendliness. They may take different forms depending on the country. In some countries, even more is required of brands, but the overall principle is the same: consider what consumers might think after reading or hearing a climate promise. If there is even the slightest possibility that they could interpret the climate promise in a wider or different sense to the one intended, the brand has the responsibility of clarifying the true meaning. Marketers must thus adapt the language they speak to consumers. This is clearly the case in Belgium, given the results of our research: 59% of the campaigns tested display one or more characteristics of greenwashing. In most cases, it's because climate-friendly promises are too vague.

HOW CONSUMERS ARE ASKING US TO ADAPT OUR LANGUAGE

We know that consumers have underlying doubts that turn into disbelief or distrust at the slightest trigger when companies talk about sustainability or climate friendliness. This is a massive issue for climate-friendly campaigns. It doesn't matter whether the company behind the campaign is a 'climate-friendly' company, 'in transition' or an old-normal company. It also doesn't matter if the campaign is 'clean', that is to say free of all greenwashing. It doesn't even matter which industry the company operates in, as proven by the research we published at the end of 2021 under the leadership of professor Verleye. We concluded that the vast majority of companies are not succeeding in credibly conveying their or their products' climate friendliness to consumers, due to the language that they're using today. "The data is clear," explains Gino Verleye, "consumers are giving off masses of indicators that show that they are highly suspicious." More than nine in ten Belgians (94%) wonder whether companies are being honest about their climate actions, due to the credibility deficit that is clearly shown in figure 44. This credibility deficit has nothing to do with whether a company actually is, or trying to be, climate-friendly. Consumers' inherent distrust of business is the result of the numerous Dieselgates and other company scandals. "That distrust has reached historical highs, which means that all companies are affected," continues Verleye. "Only local companies are given the benefit of the doubt to start, because consumers feel that local companies can't afford to rip them off." However, only 14% of Belgians believe that multinationals are being honest when sharing a sustainability message. That number rises to 18% for SMEs and 22% if the company is specifically focused on sustainability. "The fact that even sustainable companies are struggling to come across as credible shows just how deep that doubt and distrust runs," adds Verleye.

This means that all companies, even climate-friendly companies, have to earn their credibility. They have to let their actions and products do the talking, but that's often where things go wrong. Companies regularly fail to make their climate efforts clear. No matter how hard companies are working to be more climate-friendly, they're not managing to convey that to consumers; eight in ten Belgians (81%) say that the business sector is doing too little to solve the climate problem. Our language is clearly falling short. "It seems like two different worlds: one for the business sector and one for consumers. You won't find much common ground between the two," Verleye says about the consumer feedback that he extracted from the data. At the same time, we know that consumers want the business sector to take climate leadership and lead them safely through the transition. This results in a catch-22 situation; on the one hand, consumer demand for businesses to take leadership has never been so high, but on the other hand, suspicion is so prevalent that businesses are often not believed if they do take leadership. According to Verleye, this paradox is undeniable: "There's a lot of noise in the lines of communication, but if the business sector adapts how it communicates, that noise should mostly disappear."

FIGURE 44

Few consumers believe companies when they talk about sustainability or climate friendliness

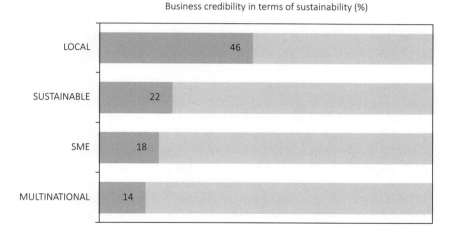

Business credibility in terms of sustainability (%)

The second part of our research into the credibility of climate-friendly campaigns also clearly showed that communications are being drowned out by background noise; those claims aren't coming through loud and clear. We tested nearly 100 campaigns by national and international brands from ten different sectors, aired for Belgian consumers on television or social networks. Those adverts shared both social and climate-friendly messages. Given that the majority of sustainable campaigns are about climate friendliness nowadays, this proportion was also reflected in the campaigns tested. Most of them talked about the climate friendliness of a company or product while a minority talked about the social aspects of sustainability.

This part of our research had three objectives. First, we wanted to know how credible campaigns were to consumers. Secondly, we wanted to find out which factors make a campaign credible. In other words, if a company wants to communicate in a credible way, how can they get consumers to hear their message? What are the various pieces of the puzzle and how do they fit together? And if we compare it to advertising regular products, are they the same puzzle pieces or do they look different? Third, we wanted to know which topics foster credibility. If consumers are asking for climate leadership, is an activist brand story better suited? Does the 'local product' story line strengthen or weaken credibility? Is a net-zero story line a strong one? These are all the questions we asked ourselves to see if we can quickly break down the credibility barrier or not.

METHODOLOGY

Research into the credibility of ads was carried out on 95 adverts that fell under the 'sustainability' tag in one way or another. 600 Belgians between 19 and 90 years old responded to 12 questions per ad in October 2021, upon request by Bilendi. Every respondent received 5 random ads to evaluate. The content of the 95 ads was also analysed using 64 characteristics that described the ad. These included certain aspects of greenwashing, creative development, the presence of specific cues and the actors on screen. Both databases were combined to feed a powerful data model. Three tasks were carried out on this data. First, we created a set of ads with which we could measure consumer response, which showed us that only 9.6% of these ads are really credible. This benchmark also serves to evaluate other/new ads. Secondly, with AMOS structural equation modelling, we could calculate an econometric model which shows the determining factors of credibility and quantifies the impact on sustainable behaviour and brand choices. Finally, this database learnt that certain ad features drive evaluation/appreciation up or down.

Less than one in ten climate-friendly campaigns are credible

"What do you do with your Nespresso capsules?" A young couple is standing in the kitchen where they've just made a Nespresso coffee. While the woman enjoys her first sip, the man removes the used capsule from the machine and throws it in the recycling bin. The voice continues: "The aluminium our capsules are made with is infinitely recyclable. That's why we like to get them back." Images then show what happens when used capsules are sent back to

Nespresso. "All the aluminium we receive gets a new life, it's used to make new products." You see thousands of capsules being processed on a conveyer belt in a factory. "Did you know that all our capsules will soon be composed of 80% recycled aluminium? Are you recycling too? Together we can make the world a little better. Drop off your capsules in store, with a delivery service or at a drop-off point." The ad ends with the well-known slogan – "What else?" – appearing on screen.

FIGURE 45

The percentage of sustainable campaigns that are credible to consumers

9.7%

of sustainable
campaigns are credible
to consumers

This is the most credible ad of the 95 that we tested. I showed it to an art director at an advertising agency, who couldn't believe that this was the new 'good'. "This doesn't respect the rules of good advertising," he said. That's right, this ad won't win prizes at large creative award shows, but that's not the benchmark anymore. The climate friendliness of a brand or product affects one of the most existential problems that humankind has ever faced. The promise that a product will help you have an impact on that existential problem is more important than the promise that a product will help you remove grease from your kitchen wall quicker. We have all seen those ads in which the most disgusting kitchen tiles become sparkling clean in just one easy wipe and we all know it's an exaggeration that would never happen in real life, but nobody is asking for their money back. Everyone also knows that this exaggerative language is not the kind of language you use to say that your product is helping solve the climate crisis. It's far too sensitive a topic for us to come in all guns blazing. Climate friendliness is first and foremost about the credibility of that climate promise, as proven by the results of our study. "60% of a consumer's motivation to choose a climate-friendly product, instead of the regular alternative, is determined by how credible its advertising is," says Verleye. "It's thus fundamental for campaigns to be credible. Only then can they fulfil their purpose and help influence product choices." What was seen as good advertising in the old normal is thus not necessarily good in the new normal. Good, in the climate normal, above all means credible.

With that in the back of our minds, the next question of course is how credible the near-100 campaigns we tested are. The results are disconcerting: only 9.7% of them were believed by consumers. Less than one in ten campaigns succeeded in overcoming that credibility barrier. Nine in ten didn't. That's why so many consumers say that they don't see enough effort being made by the business sector. Even if that effort is being made, consumers don't believe it. There's not much difference between sectors. We can conclude, for example, that credibility isn't necessarily a bigger problem for sectors with higher carbon emissions (see figure 46). Gino Verleye explains: "We are clearly dealing with a language issue. If our objective is to be credible, we're not approaching it in the right way."

FIGURE 46

The proportion of credible campaigns per sector (%)

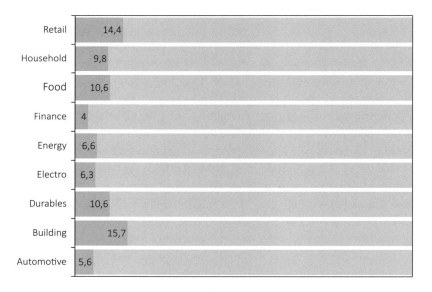

This credibility problem prevents us from accomplishing a number of tasks. First, companies are struggling to increase sales of climate-friendly products and thus ensure the resulting growth. Second, this lack of credibility slows

WE ARE DEALING WITH A LANGUAGE PROBLEM

—————

a company's transition to becoming a climate-friendly company that is part of the solution. Third, consumers are under the impression that companies don't want to take up the mantle of social leadership, which serves not only to increase their cynicism, but also their climate anxiety. Who will take the lead if it's not government or business? What is, as such, an advertising problem has repercussions on a much larger scale.

On the other hand, we know the power that advertising can have. Adverts can move mountains for the company behind the ad and sometimes even succeed in making a cultural difference. Felix Creutzig said that climate friendliness must become the social norm, which would serve the business sector well in both the short and long-term. Advertising can make it the norm. But what language do we need to use and which words and story lines are best suited?

The five drivers of credible, climate-friendly advertising
We were able to deduce a lot of information from observing consumer reactions to the 95 sustainable campaigns we tested. As a result, we identified five factors that determine the credibility of a climate-friendly campaign. These five factors explain 72% of the differences between the credibility scores of the various campaigns, which points to two things. "First, it shows the scientific validity of the model," explains Gino Verleye. "In social sciences, a model is valid if it explains more than 30% of a score." Secondly, it makes it easy for companies to understand what they need to do in order to be credible. These five factors create a sort of 'Safe Advertising Space' in which climate-friendly products can be promoted, sustainable activities can be shared and net-zero plans revealed.

We were also able to measure the effect of the model on consumer motivations to buy in a more climate-friendly way. The aim of climate-friendly advertising is naturally to strengthen this motivation. We found that the credibility of a campaign and its score across the five drivers explains 60% of consumer motivation. Credible communication does thus have an impact. The same goes for, intent to buy. Naturally, climate-friendly advertising aims to increase consumers' intent to buy. An advert's credibility and its score across the five driving factors explained 30% of intent to buy. Other factors that influence intent to buy are price and perception of quality. As shown in figure 47, the five drivers have varying degrees of importance. Gino Verley explains: "As we saw in the regression analysis, the conclusion is that honesty bears the most weight.

SPEAK UP NOW 171

FIGURE 47

The drivers defining the credibility of climate- friendly advertising

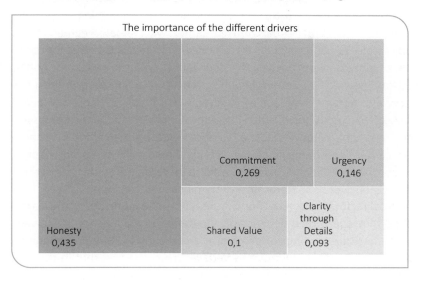

The importance of the different drivers

Commitment
0,269

Urgency
0,146

Honesty
0,435

Shared Value
0,1

Clarity
through
Details
0,093

! Honesty or transparency doesn't mean that the company itself finds that it is being honest, but rather whether the customer feels that what is being said in the ad is honest."

! The second most important factor is the company's commitment. We measured the extent to which a company succeeds in demonstrating its commitment rather than how committed the company actually is. "Some climate-friendly companies are strongly committed but talk about it in the language of the old normal. We've noted that this doesn't work, which is a drawback for those kinds of companies," explains Verleye.

! The third factor that plays a role is whether a company is able to show that it understands the urgency of the climate crisis. "This was a surprise, but it is an important factor," Verleye continued. The background is simple: the story of the climate crisis is that we are too late, that politicians are taking decisions too slowly or not at all and that the business sector is taking too long to get off the ground. Consumers thus feel like not everyone understands the urgency of the situation. They want to know whether a company understands that urgency and is acting on it, which naturally fits into the framework of consumers demanding that the business sector take social leadership on the climate crisis. "If the ad doesn't give the impression that the company understands the urgency of the climate crisis, then it's missing an important credibility factor," concluded Verleye.

! The fourth driver is 'shared value'. Gino Verleye explains: "We noticed that consumers have a clear opinion on how much action an industry is or is not taking to solve the climate problem. They form this opinion based on what they think the industry should be doing. That's something we severely underestimate; it's on this basis that consumers will evaluate whether a company creates enough value for them or not." Our data shows that the value of a solution can vary for consumers depending on the brand. In the coffee industry, how companies work with farmers in the South becomes more important sustainability factor. However, when it comes to brands selling their coffee in pods, the recyclability of the aluminium in those capsules is a very important. What we need to realise is that consumers think they know how certain industries and certain brands should solve certain problems," specifies Verleye, "and the extent to which a brand demonstrates that in their adverts and lives up to those ideas determines their credibility."

! The final factor that determines the credibility of a campaign is the clarity of the message, which depends on the details or evidence that is given. "Consumers are looking for proof of the company's willingness to act to tackle the climate problem," says Verleye. "They can find that in the carbon neutrality of a product, new packaging that is completely recyclable or the act of planting trees." Traditionally, advertising professionals and marketers are trained to simplify their messages, which must be cut down to the absolutely essential key message and brought to the consumer in as simple a way as possible. Too many details are too be avoided. But that's the old normal. In the new climate normal, details are very important.

These five drivers make a whole

These five determining factors are indivisible (see figure 48). If a company demonstrates a great deal of commitment but provides few details as to how they will actually fulfil that commitment, they cannot assume that they will achieve a high credibility score just because 'commitment' is a more important factor than 'clarity'. This is a problem facing many launches of net-zero plans: a lot of attention is paid to the promise of being climate-neutral by 2050, but there is deafening silence about how that will actually be achieved. As we can see in figure 48, the different factors are all highly dependent on each other. All the determining factors influence credibility but also influence each other. Some drivers also have a direct impact on consumers' motivation to buy climate-friendly items and their intent to buy. If a company wants to communicate in a credible way, it needs to take these five factors into account, thinking about how consumers recognise and experience the message communicated in climate-friendly ads.

FIGURE 48

All the determining factors are interconnected

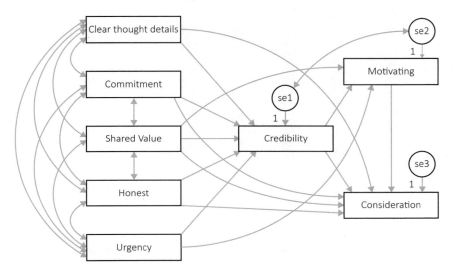

The fact that these five factors determine 72% of the credibility score of a climate-friendly advertising campaign is good news. This means that there are other determining factors to be found, although their impact on credibility is very small, and that the use of these five will ensure that climate-friendly communication is credible. As a result, companies only need to focus on these five. In so doing, they can assume that their communication will come across as credible and thus remove that first barrier preventing them from doing their job. This was proven by the analysis of the most credible, climate-friendly adverts of the 100 tested. We call it the 9.7 benchmark, the 9.7% of campaigns that consumers deemed very credible. For the purpose of clarity, we scored these ads between zero and five in terms of performance. They all scored high across all five determining factors (see figure 49). This means that these ads come across as very honest and convincingly committed, they show that the brand understands the urgency, put forward solutions that consumers also have in mind and provide enough details to show that it is a good solution. The result is a top score for credibility and a high score in terms of consumer motivation and intent to buy.

FIGURE 49

How the most credible adverts score

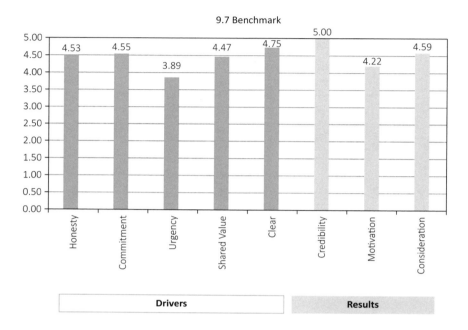

"This is the language of climate-friendly communication in the new normal," explains Verleye. This means that we need to change, as it's not the language we're used to speaking in advertising. We've also noticed this in our research. "Some brands score highly for one campaign while another campaign will fare badly," says Verleye. "This shows that companies don't master the new language and that it is more a question of luck than skill when it comes to making communications credible today." If we plot the ads of the 9.7 benchmark on a 'communication ladder', we notice that they mostly start by explaining the factual characteristics of their products, known as 'attributes', to later make the climate-friendly 'benefit' clear to consumers (see figure 50). A Belgian food retailer that used its campaign to promote its local products successfully obtained a high score for 'honesty' because it gave facts – the ad began with the exact number of local producers they work with. That number was impressive and gave them the credibility they needed to then talk about how healthy their range is.

A footwear brand's ad that scored high for 'Commitment' showed the process of creating a product containing less plastic in detail. In the old normal, we would ask ourselves what on earth they were thinking showing the consumer the whole underlying thought process of a product. We would also avoid talking through the process because it's too much like self-congratulation (a member of the management team even appears in the ad!). However, that's not the case in the climate normal. In the new normal, showing the process is an effective way of illustrating a brand's commitment. Moreover, a furniture chain scored high for 'Urgency' because they gave a list of 16 tips on how you can lead a more climate-friendly lifestyle by using their products at home. 16! In the old normal, a script like that would never have been presented to the advertiser. In the new normal, however, it shows that the company understands how urgent the climate problem is and how someone can help contribute to the solution from the comfort of their own home.

FIGURE 50

The communication ladder

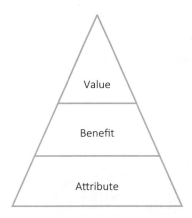

Of course, we also have the most credible ad of all, the one we talked about earlier that exposed the recycling process of coffee capsules step by step. In the old normal, we wouldn't have found that inspiring. In the new normal, it's important for consumers to know what is done with their used capsules so that they can be sure they are having an impact by recycling them. These are all examples from the 9.7 benchmark that are based on 'attributes'. Among the 95, some ads used big words and lots of ambition to capitalise on 'Value'. These did not score well in terms of credibility. What consumers want to hear today are the facts that underpin how a company is contributing to the solution, which thus responds to their call for companies to take social leadership of the climate problem and help consumers themselves have a greater positive impact.

Our research showed that less than one in ten campaigns are credible, meaning that nine in ten are not. How can the majority that don't score well improve their score? First, they can test their campaigns for the five determining factors. As we can see in figure 51, companies can establish how well their campaign scores compared to campaigns from the 9.7 benchmark, the industry they belong to and, if they want, their competitors. This food industry brand, for example, scores below the benchmark but above the industry average. It's useful for brands to compare themselves to the rest of their industry because they can find out on which factors they tend to score better. By comparing themselves to the benchmark, they can understand what else they can do to be more credible.

FIGURE 51

The scores of an advert for a climate-friendly food product compared to the 9.7 benchmark and the average score in the food industry

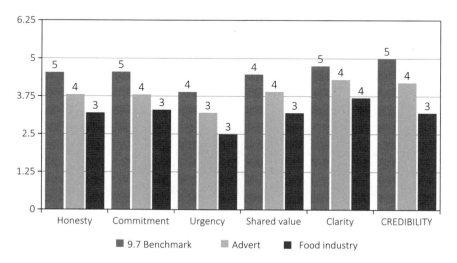

Which story lines are the most credible?

In the new climate normal, it's logical that some old story lines are less effective and that newer story lines tend to work better. Our hypothesis was that adverts with an 'activist' story line would score highly, given that consumers are expecting brands and companies to take climate leadership today. It is likely this will be reflected in the results. Another hypothesis was that the 'organic' story line would do less well. The fact that organic products are healthy is common knowledge, but whether they're climate-friendly or not is not so clear cut for consumers.

FIGURE 52

% of ads scored 'very' high by consumers

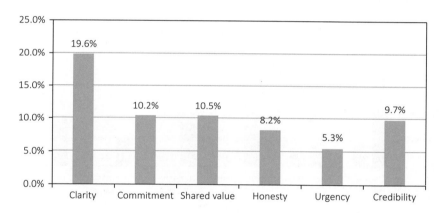

How do we know whether a story line scored well or not? To start, we took the results of all the adverts we tested and picked out the top scores for each determining factor, as shown in figure 52. These results revealed that 19.6% of ads were identified as 'very' clear by the test panel, 10.2% were 'very' committed, 10.5% had 'high' shared value, 8.2% were seen as 'very' honest and 5.3% showed 'very strong' understanding of the urgency. On that basis, we identified ads that shared the same story line, for example all adverts with an 'activist' story line, and compared them to those with a different story line. This comparison allowed us to assess the extent to which a particular story line influences credibility or not.

The 'organic' story line

Let us begin with a story line from the old normal, the organic story line. The analysis in figure 53 clearly shows that placing substantial emphasis on the organic features of a product is more likely to harm climate-friendly credibility than strengthen it. We can logically deduce this from the results, which show that the organic story line doesn't score higher than ads with different story lines for any of the five determining factors. This low score is easily comprehensible given the doubts about organic agriculture and whether it is good for the planet and climate or not. It's a typical example of an old story line, the merits of which reside uniquely in the old normal.

FIGURE 53

Evaluation of the organic story line

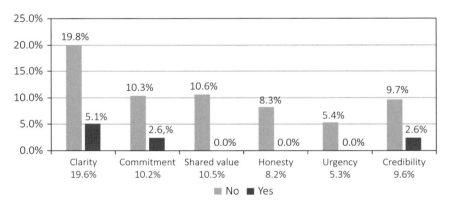

The 'local' story line

On the contrary, the local story line works well (see figure 54). The data shows that focusing on the proximity of a product, the production chain, the location of suppliers or other local characteristics generates a higher score across the board than stories without this local focus. The scores for 'clarity' (26.1%) and 'shared value' (17.8%) are significantly higher.

Does this mean that all ads must include local stories? Of course not, that would be greenwashing. Nevertheless, if there are any doubts as to which climate-friendly characteristic should feature in the ad and the product's local nature can be shared and displayed in numbers, choosing the local story line is a good option.

FIGURE 54

Evaluation of the 'local' storyline

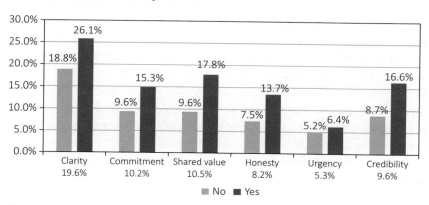

The 'activist' story line

Another story line that has a positive impact across all five factors is the activist story line. In the business sector, there is a lot of uncertainty about the value of positioning oneself as an activist. Many companies are against it because they don't feel like activists themselves or because they are worried of getting a negative reaction from their customers. They assume that they would receive some positive feedback, but mostly negative consumer reactions if they take a clear climate stance. The research we carried out for *De Duurzame Belg* has already shown us that consumer reactions are to be expected but that the positive ones will largely win through. We must not forget that consumers want companies to take more action; it's the consumer asking.

FIGURE 55

Evaluation of the 'activist' story line

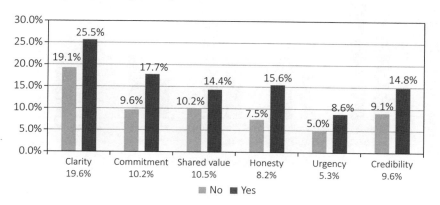

Of course, it also depends on how we define activism. Of the ads we tested, the ones that score highly are those by Ikea, Patagonia, Alpro, Triodos and Timberland. These are all, unsurprisingly, 'climate-friendly companies' that are taking their social responsibility seriously and making that commitment common knowledge. All too often, we equate an activist story line with sounding like a climate group or NGO: sharp, loud and sometimes aggressive. But that's obviously not the case. Ikea, Patagonia and Triodos sound determined in their communications and leave absolutely no room for anyone to doubt their stance on certain topics, but they're never sharp or aggressive. An activist story line (as exemplified by the aforementioned companies) contributes to higher scores across the board (figure 55). The scores for 'honesty' and 'commitment' jump by 8%, while the credibility of these ads rises by almost 6%. It's thus a story line that works well in the new climate normal, which is no surprise given that we know that 83% of consumers want the business sector to take climate leadership.

The 'biodiversity' story line
The biodiversity story line also works well in the new climate normal, scoring well across all five determining factors. This includes story lines that clearly show that a product or brand is produced with respect for nature or that brands are making efforts to restore ecosystems. A good example is Lacoste and their 'Save the Species' campaign, selling polo shirts featuring logos of various endangered animal species.

FIGURE 56

Evaluation of the 'biodiversity' story line

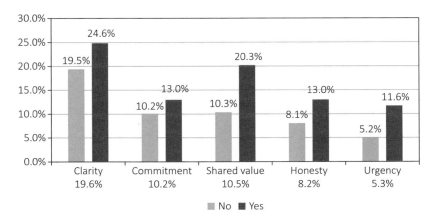

The 'climate leadership' story line

Another story line with a good success rate is climate leadership, which is substantially different to the activist story line. Velux's 'Lifetime Carbon Neutral' campaign is not activist but shows a company that is taking climate leadership and thereby responding to consumer demand. Campaigns by food retailers also tend to have high leadership content. It's thus no surprise that leadership has a positive impact across the board and helps increase the credibility score.

FIGURE 57

Evaluation of the 'climate leader' storyline

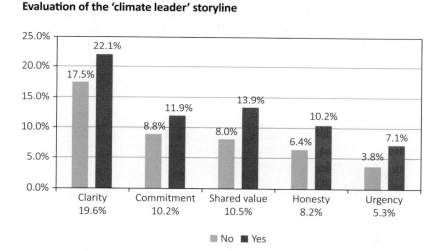

The 'partnership' story line

This is a good example of how the old version of a story scores poorly in the new normal, while the new version scores better; it's the difference between using climate labels or partnerships to give credibility to your story. We've used labels for a long time. However, we now know that consumers are questioning the credibility of certain labels (not the Fairtrade label, EU labels or Ecoscore) and that is reflected in their performance. Companies that want to earn their credibility through labels tend to score lower than companies that base their credibility on partnerships, which tend to score above average. Building partnerships, like Velux's collaboration with the WWF, is thus much more suited to the new climate normal than the use of labels.

FIGURE 58

Evaluation of the 'label' versus 'partnership' story line

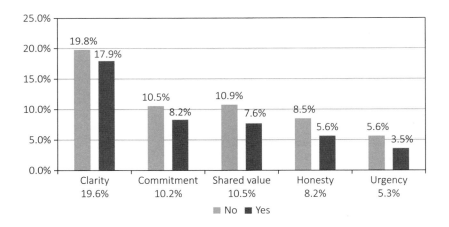

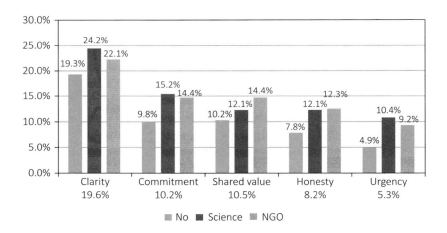

THIS WILL BE GREATER THAN ANYTHING WE HAVE EVER SEEN. EVERY LIVING THING WILL BE AFFECTED

SPEAK UP NOW

"People do not understand the magnitude of what is going on. This will be greater than anything we have ever seen in the past. This will be unprecedented. Every living thing will be affected."[148] That's Katharine Hayhoe speaking, chief scientist for the Nature Conservancy in the US and professor at Texas Tech University. "Our infrastructure, worth trillions of dollars, built over decades, was built for a planet that no longer exists," she continues. "Changing that infrastructure would cost further trillions, so allowing greenhouse gas emissions to continue to grow would mean ever-rising impacts and costs. The whole of modern life is at stake. Human civilisation is based on the assumption of a stable climate. But we are moving far beyond the stable range."

Scientists are speaking out, louder and more frequently than ever. All of them are giving the world the same warning: there is no more time for incremental change, only drastic change will do now. The climate and biodiversity crisis is a very abstract topic, complex and impossible for one person to fully comprehend. It's thus easy to think that it won't be all that bad or that we can't actually do a lot about it. Some people master the problem completely and devote their lives to finding solutions. These are the people who write the IPCC reports and I've been lucky to speak with a number of them. One reflected on how people would look back at us in 2200. For them, our present day would be 178 years in the past. For us, it would be like looking back at people in 1844, when Samuel Morse sent the first telegram, Giuseppe Verdi's opera *Hernani* premiered in Venice and the 11th president of the US was sworn in. We find it hard to envision life in 1844. People in 2200 thinking about us will feel the same way, unless we fail to implement the Paris Agreement or achieve the targets of the SDGs. If we fail, they will well and truly know who we are: the people who messed it all up, making them live in a world with an unstable climate that is nothing like the Holocene. Who wants to be responsible for that? Nobody, I hope.

What can you do about it as a marketer? A lot, according to Felix Creutzig. He showed that consumers can significantly help us reduce emissions, but we can only achieve those emissions cuts if we make climate-friendly consumption the social norm. 'Climate-friendly' companies are showing us how to do that.

Nevertheless, despite our best efforts, consumers feel that they are hearing nothing but silence from the business sector. That is not what they expect of us. They expect us to take leadership, to speak up and guide society safely through the sustainability transition. We now know that it's about the language we speak. We won't get through to them speaking the language of the old normal, because promoting climate-friendly products in the same way as regular products doesn't work. The government thinks we need to be much stricter on ourselves and is imposing new rules. They're not wrong, given the high urgency of the climate problem. Luckily we know what the language of the new climate normal sounds like and we can build our credibility as a brand that's part of the solution. We have seen that this is what companies need to focus on if they want to be successful in the near future.

Marketers and advertising professionals have all the tools they need to make their subsequent campaigns a climate-friendly success that builds rather than destroys a company's credibility.

Let's close with three very practical final thoughts.

Make all campaigns net-zero
We have enough tools at our fingertips to ensure that both the production and distribution of advertising is net-zero. Today, it's still impossible to achieve this without quite a lot of offsetting, but we will get there. We will reach a point where we can reduce the emissions produced by campaigns by 90%. In any case, it's so easy to cut emissions today that it's a conscious choice not to do so.

Reduce the emissions caused by you doing your job well
If you speak the right language, your climate promises will become more credible but that doesn't mean there will be no more problems. All you did was provide a solution to the credibility deficit your company was dealing with, which ensures that your campaigns are more effective. However, you also need to take responsibility for the emissions produced by the additional sales generated thanks to your campaigns. The first step is to quantify those emissions. It's quite simple to work out, if you know how many additional

sales can be directly linked to your campaign and the total emissions of the product you're selling (over its full life cycle):

Number of extra products sold x total emissions per product = "advertising emissions"

Once you've calculated your advertising emissions, you can type that number into an emissions comparison site, which will calculate how many trips around the world would generate the same emissions, how many times you can fly from New York to London and so on. The results will make you fall off your chair. That's when you know there's still work to be done. Subsequent campaigns may generate even higher emissions, in which case the company would be actively making the climate problem worse. Companies must ask themselves how they can cut those emissions but the answer is not easy. Do we want to make campaigns for products we know we can't reduce the total emissions of? Shouldn't we limit ourselves to making campaigns to promote low-emissions products? Is it still okay to promote meat products? Is it still responsible to advertise diesel cars? Unless you work for a 'climate-friendly' company, this question is impossible to answer today. Everybody knows that it's better not to promote these products but the company's reality forces our hand. One answer is to align 'advertising emissions' with the company's net-zero plan. A net-zero plan must ensure that the total emissions of all products are drastically reduced.

Take the planet with you to every meeting

Invite the planet to take part in every meeting and give it a seat at the head of the meeting table (our planet is available to purchase as a blow-up globe). Make sure that its voice is heard in every discussion and decision. Only by gaining the planet's agreement can you take a step closer to implementing the Paris Agreement and the SDGs, no matter how small a step it is. For your brand or company, it's a step in the right direction to becoming part of the solution. If no-one knows the answer, research the impact that a decision could have. Conversely, if everyone knows that you're on the verge of taking a decision that the planet wouldn't agree with and you go ahead regardless, then you know that you're actively contributing to the climate problem and that you're letting your company take a step backwards, as part of the problem. Someone in the meeting room is sure to say that there's nothing that can be done about it, that the numbers need to be made, that there's no time to do things differently, that it's not all that important because the impact will be small anyway and so on. In that case, take the floor as a climate-friendly marketer and cite James Watt from BrewDog: "The scientific consensus is clear: we are sleepwalking off the edge of a cliff." Who today wants to take responsibility for making the climate problem worse, even if just by a little?

Let's get to work now.
The climate can wait no longer.

"NOW IS THE TIME TO SPEAK UP FOR SILENCE IS DOING NOTHING."

Acknowledge-
ments.

A book can only become a reality thanks to the help of all the people who make it possible. My greatest thanks go to my wife, Heidi Lagast. This book would never have been completed without her patience, coaching, moral support and pen. Thank you to Hermine Van Coppenolle, my step-daughter, who's writing her doctorate about the Paris Agreement and, in doing so, is trying to unravel what the impact of different countries' climate ambitions will be (I'm so proud!). Thank you for the inspiration, information and permission to share your until-now unpublished scientific work on net-zero targets.

This book is based on the book *De Duurzame Belg* and the related scientific research on the credibility of climate-friendly advertising. This would never have happened without the scientific leadership of professor Gino Verleye at the University of Ghent and collaboration with my colleague Inez Schoenaers at Bubka. Marie Anne Stevens from Nielsen Media and the people at Bilendi also leant a strong helping hand.

The scientific insights into the climate crisis and the changing climate came from conversations with professor Felix Creutzig (Berlin Institute of Technology), Johan Rockström (Potsdam Institute for Climate Impact Research), Damon Centola (University of Pennsylvania) and Tom Cernev (Centre for the study of existential risk).

I also want to thank my partners at Bubka for their patience, brainstorming sessions and feedback: Raf Van Raemdonck, Ben Van Asbroek, Caro Peeters, Dirk Malfliet and Michel Laukens.

Finally, a big thank you to my 89-year-old mother, Fabienne Waelput, who is sure to see me more often now.

Notes.

1   *Tree-planting punks: First carbon-negative beer business.* (2020, 7 September). Zureli. Last accessed on 12 June 2022, at https://www.zureli.com/tree-planting-punks-first-carbon-negative-beer-business/

2   Goering, L. (2021, 13 November). *"Architects of desire": Can advertising agencies glamorise climate solutions?* Reuters. Last accessed on 24 June 2022, at https://www.reuters.com/business/cop/architects-desire-can-advertising-agencies-glamorise-climate-solutions-2021-11-13/

3   Chin-A-Fo, H. N. H. (2020, 19 February). *De goden kunnen niet meer oversteken.* De Standaard. Last accessed on 24 June 2022, at https://www.standaard.be/cnt/dmf20200218_04854798

4   Editors of EarthSky. (2017, 3 September). *Dark for 2 years after dino-killing asteroid? | Earth | EarthSky.* EarthSky | Updates on Your Cosmos and World. Last accessed on 24 June 2022, at https://earthsky.org/earth/dino-killing-asteroid-2-years-darkness-ncar-study/

5   Yeo, W. (2016, 11 February). *With 99 Percent Confidence: Senator Timothy E. Wirth and the Hansen Hearing of 1988.* Digital Maryland. Last accessed on 26 June 2022, at https://collections.digitalmaryland.org/digital/collection/saac/id/50486/

6   Grist. (2021, 5 April). *A look back at James Hansen's seminal testimony on climate, part two.* Last accessed on 26 June 2022, at https://grist.org/article/a-climate-hero-the-testimony/

7   *Earth Summit (1992) | Encyclopedia.com.* (n.d.). Encyclopedia.Com. Last accessed on 26 June 2022, at https://www.encyclopedia.com/environment/energy-government-and-defense-magazines/earth-summit-1992

8   Kolbert, E. (2015, 17 August). *The Woman Who Could Stop Climate Change.* The New Yorker. Last accessed on 26 June 2022, at https://www.newyorker.com/magazine/2015/08/24/the-weight-of-the-world

9   Greene, B. (2016, 17 February). *Impossible isn't a fact; it's an attitude: Christiana Figueres at TED2016.* TED Blog. Last accessed on 26 June 2022, at https://blog.ted.com/impossible-isnt-a-fact-its-an-attitude-christiana-figueres-at-ted2016/

10 *The evidence is clear: the time for action is now. We can halve emissions by 2030.* (2022, 4 April). IPCC. Last accessed on 30 May 2022, at https://www.ipcc.ch/2022/04/04/ipcc-ar6-wgiii-pressrelease/

11   Environmental and Energy Study Institute (EESI). (n.d.). *Fossil Fuels | EESI*. EESI. Last accessed on 30 May 2022, at https://www.eesi.org/topics/fossil-fuels/description

12   Hook, L. (2022, 9 May). *World on course to breach global 1.5C warming threshold within five years*. Financial Times. Last accessed on 30 May 2022, at https://www.ft.com/content/6f73668d-ce55-4e23-a8a7-340e316f555c?shareType=nongift

13   Sarkar, S. (2022, 19 April). *India experiences its hottest March in 122 years*. Quartz. Last accessed on 25 June 2022, at https://qz.com/india/2156332/india-experiences-its-hottest-march-in-122-years/?utm_source=email&utm_medium=daily-brief&utm_content=93b2fce2-c02a-11ec-bf4a-8e13348e5887

14   Verma, S. (2022, 3 May). *The heat in Delhi is unbearable. This is what the climate crisis feels like*. Climate Home News. Last accessed on 26 June 2022, at https://www.climatechangenews.com/2022/04/29/the-heat-in-delhi-is-unbearable-this-is-what-the-climate-crisis-feels-like/

15   Room, P. (2022, June 17). Can we ever Rouse people about global warming? Age of Aquarius Daily News. https://aoadailynews.com/can-we-ever-rouse-people-about-global-warming/

16   MELLOR, S. (2022, 30 April). *Impossible to work after 10 o'clock in the morning': India swelters in hottest March in 122 years*. Fortune. Last accessed on 3 May 2022, at https://fortune.com/2022/04/20/india-swelters-in-hottest-march-in-122-years/

17   *Climate Forward: Less water forever*. (n.d.). NYT. Last accessed on 25 June 2022, at https://messaging-custom-newsletters.nytimes.com/template/oakv2?campaign_id=54&emc=edit_clim_20220429&instance_id=59986&nl=climateforward&productCode=CLIM®i_id=105290677&segment_id=90809&te=1&uri=nyt%3A%2F%2Fnewsletter%2F109a913c-ec52-522b-ba81-426c0434b-2b3&user_id=5abe715846fac60a7038ba8d84d179bc

18   Hancock, A. (2022, 23 August). *Almost half of Europe under drought warning conditions*. Financial Times. Last accessed on 23 August 2022, at https://www.ft.com/content/2c10693b-49f2-40db-a0c0-b46e3f706dbf

19   Lombrana, L. M. (2021, 8 July). *Climate Change Linked to 5 Million Deaths a Year, New Study Shows*. Bloomberg. Last accessed on 8 March 2022, at https://www.bloomberg.com/news/articles/2021-07-07/climate-change-linked-to-5-million-deaths-a-year-new-study-shows#xj4y7vzkg

20   Wim Vermeulen. (2020, 12 December). *Worldwide premiere of "The Decade of Action"* [Video]. YouTube. https://www.youtube.com/watch?v=yCuheTKZA88

21   Spokes, M. (2021, 16 April). *'The New Climate War': Michael E. Mann on how to fight the climate inactivists*. The Oxford Blue. Last accessed on 31 May 2022, at https://www.theoxfordblue.co.uk/2021/04/16/the-new-climate-war-michael-e-mann-on-how-to-fight-the-climate-inactivists/

22 Ramelli, S., Ossola, E., & Rancan, M. (2021). Stock price effects of climate activism: Evidence from the first Global Climate Strike. *Journal of Corporate Finance, 69*, 102018. https://doi.org/10.1016/j.jcorpfin.2021.102018

23 Wikipedia contributors. (2022, 3 June). *September 2019 climate strikes*. Wikipedia. Last accessed on 26 June 2022, at https://en.wikipedia.org/wiki/September_2019_climate_strikes

24 Ramelli, S., Ossola, E., & Rancan, M. (2021). Stock price effects of climate activism: Evidence from the first Global Climate Strike. *Journal of Corporate Finance, 69*, 102018. https://doi.org/10.1016/j.jcorpfin.2021.102018

25 Ortiz, I., Burke, S., Berrada, M., & Cortés, S. H. (2021). *World Protests: A Study of Key Protest Issues in the 21st Century* (1st ed. 2022 ed.). Palgrave Macmillan.

26 Taylor, A. (2021, 4 November). *Why is the world protesting so much? A new study claims to have some answers*. The Washington Post. Last accessed on 2 June 2022, at https://www.washingtonpost.com/world/2021/11/04/protests-global-study/

27 *Laurence on*. (n.d.). Twitter. Last accessed on 31 May 2022, at https://twitter.com/Lill_1971/status/1512720127627825159

28 Godin, M. (2022, 29 March). *Farhana Yamin's Journey From Climate Summits to Street Protests*. The New York Times. Last accessed on 26 June 2022, at https://www.nytimes.com/2022/03/29/climate/farhana-yamin-climate.html?referringSource=articleShare

29 *Our Positions and Demands – Scientist Rebellion*. (n.d.). Scientistrebellion.Com. Last accessed on 26 June 2022, at https://scientistrebellion.com/our-positions-and-demands/

30 Redfern, J. C. M. (2022, 15 April). *Don't look away: Dr. Peter Kalmus on the United Nations' latest climate report*. Source New Mexico. Last accessed on 26 June 2022, at https://sourcenm.com/2022/04/15/dont-look-away-dr-peter-kalmus-on-the-united-nations-latest-climate-report/

31 *Peter Kalmus on*. (2022, 20 April). Twitter. Last accessed on 26 June 2022, at https://twitter.com/ClimateHuman/status/1516797155922481153

32 *'We've been trying warn you for so many decades': Nasa climate scientist breaks down in tears at protest*. (n.d.). MSN. Last accessed on 26 June 2022, at https://www.msn.com/en-gb/news/world/we-ve-been-trying-warn-you-for-so-many-decades-nasa-climate-scientist-breaks-down-in-tears-at-protest/ar-AAWbPpW

33 Rogiers, F. (2022, 19 April). *Lang genoeg beleefd geweest, vindt de klimaatwetenschapper*. De Standaard. Last accessed on 26 June 2022, at https://www.standaard.be/cnt/dmf20220418_97218852

34 White, N. (2022, 4 April). *A Paris Agreement Architect Is Now Terrified by Lack of Climate Action*. Bloomberg. Last accessed on 26 June 2022, at https://www.bloomberg.com/tosv2.html?vid=&uuid=e369d826-f520-11ec-90ba-724f48434667&url=L25ld3MvYXJ0aWNsZXMvMjAyMi0wNC0wNC9pcGNjLXJlcG9ydC1sYWNrLW9mLWNsaW1hdGUtYWN0aW9uLWltbW9yYWwtc2F5cy1jaHJpc3RpYW5hLWZpZ3VlcmVz

35   Harvey, F. (2022a, April 6). *IPCC report: 'now or never' if world is to stave off climate disaster*. The Guardian. Last accessed on 26 June 2022, at https://www.theguardian.com/environment/2022/apr/04/ipcc-report-now-or-never-if-world-stave-off-climate-disaster

36   https://www.dailymail.co.uk/news/article-10214365/Insulate-Britain-eco-zealot-goes-HUNGER-STRIKE-jailed-roadblocking-protest.html

37   *'On Easter Sunday I was alone in a cell'*. (2022, 27 April). Christian Climate Action. Last accessed on 26 June 2022, at https://christianclimateaction.org/2022/04/27/on-easter-sunday-i-was-alone-in-a-cell/

38   Taylor, M., Holden, E., Collyns, D., Standaert, M., & Kassam, A. (2021, 25 August). *The young people taking their countries to court over climate inaction*. The Guardian. Last accessed on 26 June 2022, at https://www.theguardian.com/environment/2021/may/07/the-young-people-taking-their-countries-to-court-over-climate-inaction

39   Gallagher, T. (2022, 12 January). *Climate change on trial: The European countries taking their governments to court*. Euronews. Last accessed on 26 June 2022, at https://www.euronews.com/green/2021/06/17/climate-change-is-on-trial-all-the-countries-taking-their-governments-to-court

40   Harrabin, B. R. (2021, 14 September). *Climate change: Young people very worried – survey*. BBC News. Last accessed on 26 June 2022, at https://www.bbc.com/news/world-58549373

41   Pruitt-Young, S. (2021, 11 September). *Climate Change Is Making Natural Disasters Worse — Along With Our Mental Health*. NPR. Last accessed on 26 June 2022, at https://choice.npr.org/index.html?origin=https://www.npr.org/2021/09/11/1035241392/climate-change-disasters-mental-health-anxiety-eco-grief?t=1648389757008

42   Duggan, J., Haddaway, N. R., & Badullovich, N. (2021). Climate emotions: it is ok to feel the way you do. *The Lancet Planetary Health*, *5*(12), e854–e855. https://doi.org/10.1016/s2542-5196(21)00318-1

43   Grist. (2021b, October 3). *It's not just you: Everyone is Googling 'climate anxiety'*. Last accessed on 26 June 2022, at https://grist.org/language/climate-anxiety-google-search-trends/

44   Lawrance, E. (2021, 13 May). Spiral: The impact of climate change on mental health and emotional wellbeing: current evidence and implications for policy and practice. Imperial College London. Last accessed on 26 June 2022, at https://spiral.imperial.ac.uk/handle/10044/1/88568

45   *Global Risks Report 2022*. (n.d.). World Economic Forum. Last accessed on 30 May 2022, at https://www.weforum.org/reports/global-risks-report-2022

46   *The economics of climate change | Swiss Re*. (2022, 16 May). Swiss Re. Last accessed on 31 May 2022, at https://www.swissre.com/institute/research/topics-and-risk-dialogues/climate-and-natural-catastrophe-risk/expertise-publication-economics-of-climate-change.html

47   Flavelle, C. (2021, 4 November). *Climate Change Could Cut World Economy by $23 Trillion in 2050*. The New York Times. Last accessed on 31 May 2022, at https://www.nytimes.com/2021/04/22/climate/climate-change-economy.html

48   Dennett, C. (2022, 23 May). *Caroline Dennett on LinkedIn: #jumpship #truth-teller | 1538 comments*. LinkedIn. Last accessed on 30 May 2022, at https://www.linkedin.com/feed/update/urn:li:activity:6934409781495431168/#

49   *Climate Change Laws of the World*. (n.d.). Grantham Research Institute on Climate Change. Last accessed on 31 May 2022, at https://climate-laws.org

50   *Taking companies to court over climate change: who is being targeted?* (2022, 12 May). Grantham Research Institute on Climate Change and the Environment. Last accessed on 31 May 2022, at https://www.lse.ac.uk/granthaminstitute/news/taking-companies-to-court-over-climate-change-who-is-being-targeted/

51   Chelsea Harvey, E&E News. (2022, 7 April). *New IPCC Report Looks at Neglected Element of Climate Action: People*. Scientific American. Last accessed on 1 July 2022, at https://www.scientificamerican.com/article/new-ipcc-report-looks-at-neglected-element-of-climate-action-people/

52   Campbell, C. (2022, 20 May). *Climate graphic of the week: Historic blaze in New Mexico as extreme global weather events rise*. Financial Times. Last accessed on 3 June 2022, at https://www.ft.com/content/86a714e7-1513-489b-8318-7f167c5e51d0?desktop=true&segmentId=7c8f09b9-9b61-4fbb-9430-9208a9e-233c8#myft:notification:daily-email:content

53   *Climate Forward: No reusable cup? In Australia, it's at your own risk.* (n.d.). NYT. Last accessed on 1 July 2022, at https://messaging-custom-newsletters.nytimes.com/template/oakv2?campaign_id=54&emc=edit_clim_20220412&instance_id=58278&nl=climate-forward&productCode=CLIM®i_id=105290677&segment_id=88224&te=1&uri=nyt%3A%2F%2Fnewsletter%2F-22b730eb-4f9b-5364-a65d-1346ebc33c10&user_id=5abe715846fac60a-7038ba8d84d179bc

54   *How KeepCup became a leader in the reuse revolution*. (n.d.). Acehub. Last accessed on 1 July 2022, at https://acehub.org.au/news/how-keepcup-became-a-leader-in-the-reuse-revolution

55   Raworth, K. (2017). *Doughnut Economics: Seven Ways to Think Like a 21st-Century Economist*. Chelsea Green Publishing Company.

56   *PCC: "Now or never" on 1.5°C warming limit*. (2022, 4 April). World Meteorological Organization. https://public.wmo.int/en/media/press-release/ipcc-now-or-never-15°c-warming-limit
     Room, P. (2022, 17 June). *Can we ever Rouse people about global warming?* Age of Aquarius Daily News. https://aoadailynews.com/can-we-ever-rouse-people-about-global-warming/

57   Rockstrom, J., Gaffney, O., & Thunberg, G. (2021). *Breaking Boundaries: The Science Behind our Planet*. DK.

58 Harvey, F. (2022a, 21 March). *Heatwaves at both of Earth's poles alarm climate scientists*. The Guardian. Last accessed on 1 July 2022, at https://www.theguardian.com/environment/2022/mar/20/heatwaves-at-both-of-earth-poles-alarm-climate-scientists

59 Briggs, B. H. (2022, 8 March). *Amazon rainforest reaching tipping point, researchers say*. BBC News. Last accessed on 1 July 2022, at https://www.bbc.com/news/science-environment-60650415

60 *Biodiversity loss | What is the scale of loss? | Royal Society*. (n.d.). Royal Society. Last accessed on 1 July 2022, at https://royalsociety.org/topics-policy/projects/biodiversity/what-is-the-scale-of-biodiversity-loss/

61 *Biodiversity loss | What is the scale of loss? | Royal Society*. (n.d.). Royal Society. Last accessed on 1 July 2022, at https://royalsociety.org/topics-policy/projects/biodiversity/what-is-the-scale-of-biodiversity-loss/

62 Huber, B. (n.d.). *Report: Fertilizer responsible for more than 20 percent of total agricultural emissions*. Food and Environment Reporting Network. Last accessed on 31 May 2022, at https://thefern.org/ag_insider/report-fertilizer-responsible-for-more-than-20-percent-of-total-agricultural-emissions/

63 https://royalsociety.org/topics-policy/projects/biodiversity/what-is-the-scale-of-biodiversity-loss/

64 United Nations Office for Disaster Risk Reduction. (2022). *Global Assessment Report on Disaster Risk Reduction 2022: Our World at Risk*. Uno.

65 Mathiesen, K. (2022, 1 March). *The link between Putin and climate change*. POLITICO. Last accessed on 1 July 2022, at https://www.politico.eu/article/link-vladimir-putin-climate-change-russia-ukraine/

66 Mathiesen, K. (2022b, 1 March). *The link between Putin and climate change*. POLITICO. Last accessed on 1 July 2022, at https://www-politico-eu.cdn.ampproject.org/c/s/www.politico.eu/article/link-vladimir-putin-climate-change-russia-ukraine/amp/

67 Kennedy, C. (2021, 13 July). *Oil & Gas Share Of Russia's GDP Dropped To 15% In 2020*. OilPrice.Com. Last accessed on 1 July 2022, at https://oilprice.com/Latest-Energy-News/World-News/Oil-Gas-Share-Of-Russias-GDP-Dropped-To-15-In-2020.html

68 Kurth, T., Wübbels, G., Portafaix, A., Felde, A. M. Z., & Zielcke, S. (2021, 27 September). *The Biodiversity Crisis Is a Business Crisis*. BCG Global. Last accessed on 1 July 2022, at https://www.bcg.com/publications/2021/biodiversity-loss-business-implications-responses

69 Wim Vermeulen, Bart Lombaerts. (2020, 12 December). *Worldwide premiere of "The Decade of Action"* [Video]. YouTube. https://www.youtube.com/watch?v=y-CuheTKZA88

70   Tucker, I. (2022, 25 May). *Peter Kalmus: 'As a species, we're on autopilot, not making the right decisions'*. The Guardian. Last accessed on 31 May 2022, at https://www.theguardian.com/environment/2022/may/21/peter-kalmus-na-sa-scientist-climate-protest-interview

71   *Conscious Consumption*. (2022, 2 May). InSites Consulting. Last accessed on 1 June 2022, at https://insites-consulting.com/bookzines/conscious-consumption/?_ga=2.202369043.362827608.1654072495-1660109546.1654072494

72   Vermeulen, W., & Verleye, G. (2020). *De duurzame Belg* (1st edition). Lannoo.

73   *Sustainability: The European Story*. (n.d.). Kantar. Last accessed on 1 June 2022, at https://www.kantar.com/campaigns/sustainability-the-european-story

74   International Trade Centre (2019). The European Union Market for Sustainable Products. The retail perspective on sourcing policies and consumer demand. ITC, Geneva.

75   *2021 Sustainable Market Share Index Report | CSB Practice Forum 2022*. (2022, 13 April). [Video]. YouTube. https://www.youtube.com/watch?v=uVVBynD-g9oA&list=PLCQnroBr9V7_emIfACnfxjq1qak3ISVCY&index=10

76   *IPCC: "Now or never" on 1.5°C warming limit*. (2022, April 4). World Meteorological Organization. https://public.wmo.int/en/media/press-release/ipcc-now-or-never-15°c-warming-limit
     Room, P. (2022, June 17). *Can we ever Rouse people about global warming?* Age of Aquarius Daily News. https://aoadailynews.com/can-we-ever-rouse-people-about-global-warming/
     Sustainability: The European story. (n.d.). Kantar. Understand People. Inspire Growth. https://www.kantar.com/campaigns/sustainability-the-european-story

77   Why today's pricing is sabotaging sustainability. (n.d.). Kearney. Last accessed on 1 June 2022, at https://www.nl.kearney.com/consumer-retail/article/-/insights/why-todays-pricing-is-sabotaging-sustainability

78   *2021 Sustainable Market Share Index Report | CSB Practice Forum 2022*. (2022, 13 April). [Video]. YouTube. https://www.youtube.com/watch?v=uVVBynD-g9oA&list=PLCQnroBr9V7_emIfACnfxjq1qak3ISVCY&index=10

79   Net-Zero Challenge: The supply chain opportunity. (n.d.). World Economic Forum. Last accessed on 1 June 2022, at https://www.weforum.org/reports/net-zero-challenge-the-supply-chain-opportunity

80   Hammond, G. (2022, 3 June). *Octopus and Ilke launch clean energy scheme with no bills for householders*. Financial Times. Last accessed on 4 June 2022, at https://www.ft.com/content/b81307f1-94cc-4b0f-9b64-1ac072dfe9dd#my-ft:my-news:page

81   Van Doorn, J., Risselada, H., & Verhoef, P. C. (2021). Does sustainability sell? The impact of sustainability claims on the success of national brands' new product introductions. Journal of Business Research, 137, 182–193. https://doi.org/10.1016/j.jbusres.2021.08.032

82   London, L. (2020, 15 April). *Allbirds Is The First Fashion Brand To Label Its Car-bon Footprint Like Calories*. Forbes. Last accessed on 1 July 2022, at https://www.forbes.com/sites/lelalondon/2020/04/15/allbirds-is-the-first-fashion-brand-to-label-its-carbon-footprint-like-calories/

83   *Search for Sustainable Goods Grows by 71%*. (n.d.). World Wildlife Fund. Last accessed on 1 July 2022, at https://www.worldwildlife.org/press-releases/search-for-sustainable-goods-grows-by-71-as-eco-wakening-grips-the-globe

84   *Product carbon footprint labelling: consumer research 2020*. (2020, 31 December). The Carbon Trust. Last accessed on 1 July 2022, at https://www.carbontrust.com/resources/product-carbon-footprint-labelling-consumer-research-2020

85   Ho, S. (2021, 25 July). *Carbon Labels Could Soon Be On All 75,000 Unilever Prod-ucts*. Green Queen. Last accessed on 1 July 2022, at https://www.greenqueen.com.hk/unilever-carbon-labels-pilot/

86   *2 Minutes With . . . Ben Parker and Paul Austin of Made Thought*. (n.d.). Muse by Clio. Last accessed on 4 June 2022, at https://musebycl.io/2-minutes/2-minutes-ben-parker-and-paul-austin-made-thought

87   Hodgson, S. (2020, 10 November). *Breakthrough brands: The BrewDog market-ing strategy, promotion for punks*. Fabrik Brands. Last accessed on 1 July 2022, at https://fabrikbrands.com/breakthrough-brands-brewdog-marketing-strategy/

88   Edie Newsroom. (2020, 24 August). *Brewdog achieves 'carbon negativity', offset-ting more emissions than it generates*. Edie. Last accessed on 1 July 2022, at https://www.edie.net/brewdog-achieves-carbon-negativity-offsetting-more-emis-sions-than-it-generates/

89   *VELUX GROUP-WWF PARTNERSHIP PRESS RELEASE*. (n.d.). WWF Uganda. Last accessed on 1 July 2022, at https://www.wwfuganda.org/?32365/VELUX-GROUP-WWF-PARTNERSHIP-PRESS-RELEASE

90   *SBTi Progress Report 2021*. (n.d.). Science Based Targets. Last accessed on 1 July 2022, at https://sciencebasedtargets.org/reports/sbti-progress-report-2021

91   *Now For Nature: The Decade of Delivery*. (n.d.). CDP. Last accessed on 1 June 2022, at https://www.cdp.net/en/research/cdp-europe-reports/now-for-nature

92   *Winning the Race to Net Zero: The CEO Guide to Climate Advantage*. (n.d.). World Economic Forum. Last accessed on 30 May 2022, at https://www.weforum.org/reports/winning-the-race-to-net-zero-the-ceo-guide-to-climate-advantage

93   PricewaterhouseCoopers. (n.d.). *25th Annual Global CEO Survey –*. PwC. Last accessed on 1 July 2022, at https://www.pwc.com/ceosurvey

94   Van Coppenolle, H., Blondeel, M., & Van de Graaf, T. (2022b). Reframing the Climate Debate: The Origins and Diffusion of Net Zero Pledges. [Unpublished manuscript].

95   Spary, S. (2020, 3 March). *Shell faces ASA investigation over 'carbon neutral' claims*. Campaignlive. Last accessed on 1 July 2022, at https://www.campaign-live.co.uk/article/shell-faces-asa-investigation-carbon-neutral-claims/1675793

96   *The carbon offset market is falling short. Here's how to fix it.* (2022, 5 May). Financial Times. Last accessed on 1 July 2022, at https://www.ft.com/content/32b1a051-7de6-4594-b31b-753e78aefde1

97   Terazono, E. (2021, 1 December). *Morrisons ditches soya for insects in chicken feed to hatch carbon neutral eggs.* Financial Times. Last accessed on 2 June 2022, at https://www.ft.com/content/ce180ed3-67c5-4e47-91e3-32049866cae1

98   *Morrisons commits to Net Zero Carbon Emissions from its own operations by 2035.* (n.d.). Morrisons. Last accessed on 5 June 2022, at https://www.morrisons-corporate.com/media-centre/corporate-news/morrisons-commits-to-net-zero-carbon-emissions-from-its-own-operations-by-2035/

99   Hausfather, Z. (2022, 5 June). *Opinion | Climate Change Needs Durable Solutions. Tree Planting Isn't One.* The New York Times. Last accessed on 5 June 2022, at https://www.nytimes.com/2022/06/04/opinion/environment/climate-change-trees-carbon-removal.html

100   Edgecliffe-Johnson, A. (2021, 23 August). *Business can stop the ESG backlash by proving it's making a difference.* Financial Times. Last accessed on 5 June 2022, at https://www.ft.com/content/2e77a83b-bf88-4efb-8294-31db74db03c5

101   *From Surging Recovery to Elegant Advance: The Evolving Future of Luxury.* (2021, 20 December). Bain. Last accessed on 1 July 2022, at https://www.bain.com/insigvhts/from-surging-recovery-to-elegant-advance-the-evolving-future-of-luxury

102   dev@grandiz.com. (2020, 6 October). *Gucci to sell second hand on The RealReal.* RetailDetail EU. Last accessed on 1 July 2022, at https://www.retaildetail.eu/news/fashion/gucci-sell-second-hand-realreal/

103   https://www.gwi.com/hubfs/Downloads/Avery%20Dennison%20-%20Digital%20consumer%20behavior%20(1).pdf?utm_campaign=210519%20Link%20to%20email%20p2%7C&utm_medium=email&_hsmi=173690530&_hsenc=p2ANqtz-9wK8cn2r0hwCUF36vcNjyQ75Uz6KnDk0IGg0Nv-96vjdp62JMfSP4Ax5lORyyhSHcXySvQbzBNB6rKRiDhAah1otZHIO27KpACBSsx-M2UkzSBkKvOg&utm_content=173690530&utm_source=hs_automation

104   Vetter, D. (2020, 26 November). *This Is How Black Friday Hurts The Planet—But Attitudes Are Changing.* Forbes. Last accessed on 2 June 2022, at https://www.forbes.com/sites/davidrvetter/2020/11/24/this-is-how-black-friday-hurts-the-planet-but-attitudes-are-changing/

105   https://www.ingka.com/news/buyback-friday-gives-thousands-of-pieces-of-furniture-a-new-life/

106   *IKEA – "Buy Back" Program | Circular X.* (n.d.). Circular X. Last accessed on 2 June 2022, at https://www.circularx.eu/en/cases/23/ikea-buy-back-program

107   Dekens, S. (2022, 23 March). *Dit zijn de voordelen van koud(er) wassen.* Libelle. Last accessed on 1 July 2022, at https://www.libelle.be/thuis/voordelen-koud-wassen/

108   https://www.ariel.co.uk/en-gb/about-ariel/sustainability/your-commitment-how-you-can-save-energy

109   A. (2020, 2 October). *Reusable systems could become a multi-billion industry, unlocking opportunities for new business models and market participants.* Zero Waste Living Lab. Last accessed on 1 July 2022, at https://zerowastelivinglab.enviu.org/blogs/reusable-systems-could-become-a-multi-billion-industry-unlocking-opportunities-for-new-business-models-and-market-participants/

110   Moss, S. (2020, 23 September). *The zero-waste revolution: how a new wave of shops could end excess packaging.* The Guardian. Last accessed on 1 July 2022, at   https://www.theguardian.com/environment/2019/apr/21/the-zero-waste-revolution-how-a-new-wave-of-shops-could-end-excess-packaging

111   Joe, T. (2021, 7 July). *Unilever Is Expanding Its Refill and Reuse Program to Reduce Plastic Waste.* Green Queen. Last accessed on 1 July 2022, at https://www.greenqueen.com.hk/unilever-refill-reuse-plastic-waste/

112   *Challenger brands to watch in 2021 | The Marketing Society.* (2022, 29 May). Www.Marketingsociety.Com. Last accessed on 29 May 2022, at https://www.marketingsociety.com/think-piece/challenger-brands-watch-2021

113   (2022, 2 February). *Got NotBeef? NotCo Bites Back after Alpro Launches Not M*LK.* Vegconomist – the Vegan Business Magazine. Last accessed on 29 May 2022, at https://vegconomist.com/food-and-beverage/got-notbeef-notco-bites-back-after-alpro-launches-not-mlk/

114   *NotCo – Why Not.* (n.d.). Notco. Last accessed on 5 June 2022, at https://notco.com/us/about-us

115   Cooper, B. (2021, 25 June). *'Marketing is about doing less': An interview with the co-founders of Dash Water.* The Challenger Project | The Home of Challenger Brands. Last accessed on 29 May 2022, at https://thechallengerproject.com/blog/interview-jack-scott-alex-wright-co-founders-dash-water

116   Edwards, S. (2021, 28 September). *Tru Earth is eliminating plastic pollution, one laundry detergent jug at a time.* The Globe and Mail. Last accessed on 29 May 2022, at https://www.theglobeandmail.com/business/rob-magazine/top-growing-companies/article-tru-earth-is-eliminating-plastic-pollution-one-laundry-detergent-jug/

117   *Oatly v. LRF Mjölk: Sweden's 'Milk War' is getting udderly vicious.* (2019, 4 December). The Outline. Last accessed on 1 July 2022, at https://theoutline.com/post/8384/sweden-milk-war-oatly

118   *Each Country's Share of CO2 Emissions.* (n.d.). Union of Concerned Scientists. Last accessed on 1 July 2022, at https://www.ucsusa.org/resources/each-countrys-share-co2-emissions

119   *Oatly: Ditch Milk | WARC.* (n.d.). Warc. Last accessed on 1 July 2022, at https://www.warc.com/content/paywall/article/warc-awards-media/oatly-ditch-milk/en-GB/134286

120 Xu, X., Sharma, P., Shu, S., Lin, T. S., Ciais, P., Tubiello, F. N., Smith, P., Campbell, N., & Jain, A. K. (2021). Global greenhouse gas emissions from animal-based foods are twice those of plant-based foods. *Nature Food*, *2*(9), 724–732. https://doi.org/10.1038/s43016-021-00358-x

121 Carrington, D. (2022, 4 May). *Swapping 20% of beef for microbial protein 'could halve deforestation'*. The Guardian. Last accessed on 2 June 2022, at https://www.theguardian.com/environment/2022/may/04/swapping-20-of-beef-for-quorn-could-halve-global-deforestation

122 *2021 Sustainable Market Share Index Report | CSB Practice Forum 2022*. (2022, 13 April). [Video]. YouTube. https://www.youtube.com/watch?v=uV-VBynDg9oA&list=PLCQnroBr9V7_emIfACnfxjq1qak3ISVCY&index=10

123 Carrington, D. (2022b, May 4). *Swapping 20% of beef for microbial protein 'could halve deforestation'*. The Guardian. Last accessed on 5 June 2022, at https://www.theguardian.com/environment/2022/may/04/swapping-20-of-beef-for-quorn-could-halve-global-deforestation

124 *Sustainability & Consumer Behaviour 2021*. (n.d.). Deloitte United Kingdom. Last accessed on 1 July 2022, at https://www2.deloitte.com/uk/en/pages/consumer-business/articles/sustainable-consumer.html

125 *It's not easy being green: How can marketers make it easier for people to live sustainable lives? | WARC*. (n.d.). Warc. Last accessed on 1 July 2022, at https://www.warc.com/content/paywall/article/behavioural-architects/its-not-easy-being-green-how-can-marketers-make-it-easier-for-people-to-live-sustainable-lives/en-GB/145237

126 *Quorn: Re-thinking planning for the coming storm: How planning can help the planet, one brand at a time | WARC*. (n.d.). Warc. Last accessed on 1 July 2022, at https://www.warc.com/content/paywall/article/quorn-re-thinking-planning-for-the-coming-storm-how-planning-can-help-the-planet-one-brand-at-a-time/en-GB/138753

127 http://climbaz.com/chouinard72/graphics/page03.JPG

128 Langley, W. (2022, 1 June). *DWS chief resigns after police raid over greenwashing claims*. Financial Times. Last accessed on 2 June 2022, at https://www.ft.com/content/50f5c4a1-5ebe-40cc-a89f-2952f58ba324

129 Tett, G. (2022, 3 June). *ESG exposed in a world of changing priorities*. Financial Times. Last accessed on 3 June 2022, at https://www.ft.com/content/6356cc05-93a5-4f56-9d18-85218bc8bb0c?desktop=true&segmentId=7c8f09b9-9b61-4fbb-9430-9208a9e233c8#myft:notification:daily-email:content

130 Van Lierop, W. (2022, 3 June). *The SEC Is Fed Up With ESG Greenwashing*. Forbes. Last accessed on 3 June 2022, at https://www.forbes.com/sites/walvanlierop/2022/06/02/the-sec-is-fed-up-with-esg-greenwashing/

131   Edgecliffe-Johnson, A. (2021, 23 August). *Business can stop the ESG back-lash by proving it's making a difference.* Financial Times. Last accessed on 2 June 2022, at https://www.ft.com/content/2e77a83b-bf88-4efb-8294-31db74db03c5

132   Temple-West, P. (2022, 11 June). *SEC investigating Goldman Sachs for ESG claims.* Financial Times. Last accessed on 11 June 2022, at https://www.ft.com/content/5812ab1f-c2d4-4681-a6be-45f0befd92df#myft:my-news:page

133   Agnew, H. (2022, 21 February). *ESG: the next mis-selling scandal?* Financial Times. Last accessed on 5 June 2022, at https://www.ft.com/content/098131a1-97da-4327-aec3-c2fdc3f61cca

134   *DWS Group (@DWS_Group) | Twitter.* (2022, 5 June). [DWS]. Twitter. https://mobile.twitter.com/dws_group

135   Times, T. N. Y. (1970, 13 September). *A Friedman doctrine - The Social Responsibility Of Business Is to Increase Its Profits.* The New York Times. Last accessed on 3 June 2022, at https://www.nytimes.com/1970/09/13/archives/a-friedman-doctrine-the-social-responsibility-of-business-is-to.html

136   Gapper, J. (2022, 3 June). Greenwashing is tempting for CEOs who tell stories. Financial Times. Last accessed on 3 June 2022, at https://www.ft.com/content/40192e1b-378d-4eaa-97f2-39491d276faf?desktop=true&segmentId=7c8f09b9-9b61-4fbb-9430-9208a9e233c8#myft:notification:daily-email:content

137   McCurry, J., & Visontay, E. (2022, 28 February). *Ukraine island defenders who told Russian navy 'go fuck yourself' may still be alive.* The Guardian. Last accessed on 1 July 2022, at https://www.theguardian.com/world/2022/feb/27/ukraine-island-defenders-who-told-russian-officer-go-fuck-yourself-may-still-be-alive

138   Braithwaite, S. C. (2022, 26 February). *Zelensky defiant: Ukrainian president refuses US offer to evacuate, saying "I need ammunition, not a ride".* CNN. Last accessed on 1 July 2022, at https://edition.cnn.com/2022/02/26/europe/ukraine-zelensky-evacuation-intl/index.html

139   Mavisakalyan, A., Tarverdi, Y., & Weber, C. (2018b). Talking in the present, caring for the future: Language and environment. *Journal of Comparative Economics*, *46*(4), 1370–1387. https://doi.org/10.1016/j.jce.2018.01.003

140   Bednarek, S. (2022, 8 June). *We're joining legal action against Dutch airline KLM for greenwashing.* LinkedIn. Last accessed on 28 June 2022, at https://www.linkedin.com/posts/steffi-bednarek-9412b037_were-joining-legal-action-against-dutch-activity-6940167836245897216-0jFE?utm_source=linkedin_share&utm_medium=member_desktop_web

141   Shaw, N. (2022, 8 June). *Tesco advert banned after 171 complaints.* HullLive. Last accessed on 8 June 2022, at https://www.staffordshire-live.co.uk/news/uk-world-news/tesco-advert-banned-after-171-7179146

142 Evans, J. (2022, 8 June). *Tesco rebuked over greenwashing in adverts for plant-based food*. Financial Times. Last accessed on 8 June 2022, at https://www.ft.com/content/262012c0-9781-4d02-82af-bf575d9a8c6d

143 Ormesher, E. (2022, 24 March). *8 times brands fell foul of ASA for 'greenwashing'*. The Drum. Last accessed on 6 June 2022, at https://www.thedrum.com/news/2022/03/23/8-times-brands-fell-foul-asa-greenwashing

144 Lockwood, M. (2022, 6 June). *Environmental claims in your ads? Read this so you don't get banned for greenwashing*. The Drum. Last accessed on 6 June 2022, at https://www.thedrum.com/opinion/2022/06/06/environmental-claims-your-ads-read-so-you-dont-get-banned-greenwashing

145 Bowler, H. (2022b, April 28). *Why Innocent wants better 'greenwashing' governance after ASA ban*. The Drum. Last accessed on 6 June 2022, at https://www.thedrum.com/news/2022/04/28/why-innocent-wants-better-greenwashing-governance-after-asa-ban

146 *"Greenwashing" is rampant in online stores, consumer authorities find*. (2021, 29 January). Www.Euractiv.Com. Last accessed on 6 June 2022, at https://www.euractiv.com/section/circular-economy/news/greenwashing-is-rampant-in-online-stores-consumer-authorities-find/

147 Competition and Markets Authority. (2021, 20 September). *Green claims code: making environmental claims*. GOV.UK. Last accessed on 12 June 2022, at https://www.gov.uk/government/publications/green-claims-code-making-environmental-claims

148 Harvey, F. (2022, 1 June). *We cannot adapt our way out of climate crisis, warns leading scientist*. The Guardian. Last accessed on 2 June 2022, at https://www.theguardian.com/environment/2022/jun/01/we-cannot-adapt-our-way-out-of-climate-crisis-warns-leading-scientist?CMP=Share_iOSApp_Other

What others say about
Speak Up Now!

In this book, Vermeulen makes the compelling case that, when it comes to the climate crisis, every brand needs to speak up, because keeping silent is doing nothing. Action is what the world needs today. He shows that companies keeping silent not only heavily increase their own transition risks, but also create the perception that they are part of the problem, not the solution. Speak up now! is important to read for any marketer who is committed to help the planet and its consumers and wants to understand how to speak the language of the new climate normal.

— **PAUL POLMAN**, BUSINESS LEADER, CLIMATE AND EQUALITY
CAMPAIGNER, CO-AUTHOR OF *NET POSITIVE*

To moderate the climate crisis, the business sector must deliver. Just label-ling a product 'sustainable' is not enough. Wim Vermeulen convincingly demonstrates that advertising professionals – the architects of desire – must be part of the solution, refuse to further greenwash products, and instead lead the conversation towards true climate neutrality – which often means higher service quality, but less material quantity.

— **PROF. DR. FELIX CREUTZIG**, MERCATOR RESEARCH INSTITUTE ON
GLOBAL COMMONS AND CLIMATE CHANGE

Brand purpose advertising has had a rough ride with marketing scien-tists who argue that in general it does not drive business success. In the context of the most important purpose we face today – sustainability – Wim Vermeulen explores this challenge and reminds us that people are increasingly expecting companies to help solve the problems we face. Silence and inactivity are not options, whatever the anti-purpose pedagogues may think. Wim is rightly critical of greenwashing and demonstrates how widespread a problem it is. But he also points out that just because many companies wrongly think they can get away with incredible claims, doesn't mean that credible advertising is ineffective.

This is a must-read for marketers in any business that is committed to sustainability – and a wake-up call to the others.

— **PETER FIELD**, MARKETING CONSULTANT

An enlightening book for any marketer wondering how best to guide their brand or company through the climate transition.

— **WOUTER TORFS**, CEO, SCHOENEN TORFS

In this wonderfully written and engaging book, Vermeulen makes a robust and compelling case for the powerful role that marketers can play toward addressing the climate emergency. Anyone in the marketing and advertising field who is interested in learning how to speak the language of the new climate normal, and how to lead net-zero campaigns should read this book!

— **IOANNIS IOANNOU**, ASSOCIATE PROFESSOR OF STRATEGY AND ENTREPRENEURSHIP, LONDON BUSINESS SCHOOL

Climate change is not a political point of view, it is a fact-checked truth that will change our world for sure if we don't act now. Corporations and brands have a major impact on popular culture and therefore should be committed to be major players of mindset and behavioural change. As a leading player in the mobility and automotive field, our mission is to create wellbeing and welfare for society as a whole through sustainable mobility solutions. Wim Vermeulens message is a commitment on action driven solutions to be taken now.

— **JOSÉ FERNANDEZ**, CHIEF CUSTOMER EXPERIENCE, MARKETING AND DIGITAL OFFICER, D'IETEREN

Good and credible communication is an irrevocable part of a sustainable society. Companies and organisations with a clear climate policy need solutions to highlight their actions and to inspire others in their own way to get started. The climate crisis is one of everyone, Speak up now demonstrates this in a penetrating way.

— **MARIE DELVAULX**, DIRECTOR, THE SHIFT